gunnison county
Libraries
connect.   discover.   imagine.   learn.

Gunnison Library
307 N. Wisconsin, Gunnison, CO 81230
970.641.3485
www.gunnisoncountylibraries.org

LIFT

TOM MILLER

Copyright © 2016

Editorial Work by AnnaMarie McHargue

Cover Design by Arthur Cherry

Interior Design by Aaron Snethen

Published in Boise, Idaho by Elevate. A division of Elevate Publishing.

For more information please go to www.elevatepub.com or email us at info@elevatepub.com.

ISBN (print): 9781943425006

Printed in the United States of America.

Dedication

Lift is dedicated to Pat and Ray Miller – my parents – who taught me to expand my thinking and to hope. And to my wife, Catherine – who loves me well.

Endorsements

From Walter McFarland –

An artifact of this digital age of ours is advice. Endless advice from all directions swirling around us with little effect— at least to many people whose engagement has never been lower— their sense of powerlessness never higher. LIFT cuts through the noise with some good news: old paradigms of influence based on position and pedigree are being replaced by a new one that enables each of us to make a positive difference—if we so choose. Don't buy Lift unless you are ready to "go and do."

Walter McFarland,
Co-author of Choosing Change

From Broc Edwards –

A refreshingly different look at leadership filled with personal, real-life examples of normal people making a difference simply by how they lead. The authors skip the pretense and parables plaguing too many leadership books and use an easy, almost conversational writing style to focus in on three simple principles enabling ordinary leaders to have an impact on their world.

Broc Edwards,
Director of Talent Management

From Jimmy Taylor –

Tom Miller understands Dynamic Influence because he lives it! From the suburban streets of Fort Worth, Texas to the dusty roads of Kabul, Afghanistan, I invite you to walk with him and see how influence brings positive change to people and the communities where they live. Then use it as a catalyst for your own unique journey of impact. From entry-level employees to entrepreneurs, that's what we all long for – Dynamic Influence that leaves our world a little better than we found it.

Jimmy Taylor,
Co-Founder, Novotus

Table of Contents

Introduction

All over the world today men and women will go to work thinking they really don't matter to their company. They think that because they don't have an impressive title, a team they lead, a résumé with an Ivy League education, or a well-known last name they cannot be influential and do not have the capacity to impact positive change where they are. They believe influence and impact are for people with the right amount of pedigree, position and possessions. They believe that because, for years, our society has been saying it is so.

I think they're wrong. In fact, the reward and recognition industry, the industry in which I run my business, exists because companies all over the world think they're wrong. Companies today know people at all levels of the organization matter. They create customer satisfaction, lead product development and influence productivity. They impact the bottom line. In fact, the more people who show up engaged and ready to make positive change, the more their company, shareholders and customers win.

I named the book *Lift* because all great societal transformations begin not by destroying the current paradigm, but lifting people within that paradigm – by inspiring them, empowering them, and challenging them to create a better world.

Lift grew out of a desire to speak to something I've seen happen over my three decades in the business world – the shift from a traditional power paradigm (I call this "Static Influence") to a new paradigm that is much more accessible, open and inclusive – "Dynamic Influence."

Because while cities that follow ordinance and code are good, cities built by developing the community and empowering businesses that meet the needs of the citizens, are better.

And while companies with strong leadership are good, companies that empower their people to bring ideas, creatively solve problems, and shape their brand are better.

While classrooms led by quality teachers are good, classrooms where teachers tap into kids' hunger to learn, arm them with a challenge and free them to find solutions are better.

And while societies where the influence of powerful people can be good, societies where normal people utilize their community and make the courageous choice to add value are better.

It's pretty daunting to think about adding to the body of work typically referred to as "Leadership Books" and, in a way, I'm not trying to do that. Instead, I'm looking to inspire people to consider how they can use their natural talent, the community they bring to the table, and the choices they have in front of them to positively influence the world around them.

1

The Bomb Outside Our Building

LIFT

Just before the explosion, I walked across the kitchen of our small apartment in Herat, Afghanistan. I was there with my friend, Ross, coordinating a week-long discussion with a group of promising young Afghan leaders, exploring concepts like leadership, influence and entrepreneurship. We were about halfway through the week, and I had been surprised and encouraged by the conversations taking place as well as their openness to new ideas.

Mostly I was surprised by how much these Afghan men and women reminded me of...well...myself – they had many of the same desires and concerns I have. They think a lot about what kind of future their children will encounter. They want to create a better world to live in. In his blog, Ross once said of Afghans:

Universally, we all have the same human foundation...we are more alike than different. I experienced it in the business workshops, as the Afghan personalities sorted out just like they did with a group of 30 Texans in March. I experienced it as I heard fathers and grandfathers share dreams of education, peace, and prosperity for their children. I experienced it as I sat with American military leaders who desperately wanted their sacrifice to make a difference, while longing for home at the same time.

We are more similar than we think.

***

As I put my hand on the refrigerator handle that day, getting ready to open it and find something to have for lunch, the bomb went off outside our building.

When a bomb explodes in the movies, it goes off with a loud boom, but when that bomb went off outside our apartment in Afghanistan, it sounded more like the CRACK! of a Black Cat firecracker. It was a big sound, a sharp sound, and even though I'd never heard a bomb explode in real life, I knew immediately what had happened. I ducked my head and dropped to the floor.

Fortunately, I was in an interior room because the outside windows shattered and glass flew everywhere. Smoke and dust clouded the street and floated up past the broken apartment windows.

I waited to see what would happen next. Twenty seconds of silence. Thirty seconds. Then came the most chilling of moments – a sound emerged, the sound of one woman screaming. Her voice was like a siren. I don't know if she was hurt, or if someone she loved had been hurt, but for a few moments it was just her voice wailing somewhere in the midst of that rising cloud of dust and smoke.

Then people started shouting and yelling. Some of the voices sounded panicked while others sounded angry and demanding. I didn't hear anyone speak in English, just voices in a foreign language, and I didn't know if these were people coming to help or if it was the precursor to the bad guys doing more damage. That's when the guns started, gradual at first, one or two shots, but soon it became automatic machine gun fire. A constant barrage. It would be our unending soundtrack for the next 20 or 30 minutes.

I peeked my head out of the apartment. I needed to find Ross, so I left the third floor apartment and headed to the stairway where I encountered Ross sprinting up to find me. We didn't waste too many words as we turned and went back to the first floor where we thought it would be safer. Broken glass covered the stairs and gunfire was the only sound we heard on the way down. We went to a small, interior conference room that seemed, at the time, to be the safest place we could find shelter. A young Afghan man joined us.

I have a short video clip from when we were in that room. You can hear the gunfire going off in the background, as a thin ray of light shines in through the crack in the door. The whole building is shaking from the battle while we sit quietly on the floor, under a table, not saying a word.

Ross had been meeting with this young Afghan man who had such high hopes for his family, his business, and his country. He often stayed late after the business coaching sessions or, as he had done on that day, came early to meet with us and talk more about some of the ideas we had raised earlier.

"I'm sorry, I'm sorry, I'm sorry," he said over and over again to Ross and me as we sat on the floor in the conference room. Tears streamed down his face, not out of fear for himself, but out of a sense of shame that we were guests in his country and this terrible thing was happening while we were there. He also exuded a tangible disappointment – so many of our conversations revolved around how to build community, empower individuals and build sustainable businesses – but this explosion was the antithesis to all of that.

I remember thinking: *If this is my time to go, I'm okay with it.*

I called my wife, Catherine. I wanted to talk to her at least one more time. The call went through, but I changed my mind and quickly hung up – I didn't want to scare her. I knew she'd be able to hear the sound of the gunfire in the background. Things hadn't unfolded yet. I didn't want her to worry.

I started wondering about the bright young men and women we had met with that week – they were some of the real movers and shakers in Herat. One of the guys had a radio show; one of the women was a doctor. There were some young people with strong sales and business backgrounds. I hoped they hadn't been arriving at the time of the blast. I hoped they were all okay.

"We should probably move up to the next floor," Ross said, so the three of us made our way up to the next level, staying away from the windows. Outside, the gunfire continued. We heard rounds slam into the building. Soon we heard a helicopter circling high above, with bursts of ammunition raining down from it, blasting against the roof and into the street.

We found other people upstairs, so we joined them and waited. Most of us were Westerners, with only a few Afghans present. If one of the bombers came into the room, would he ask questions? Would he listen to what our interpreter had to say? Would he simply shoot us all? Or kidnap us and hold us for ransom? I remembered the images of western hostages I had seen on television, their eyes blindfolded, their captors holding AK-47s.

We crowded into the room together and everyone stayed quiet, listening, hoping for the gunshots to end. Was the attack aimed at us? There were other western organizations on our block. If we were the target, were the attackers still looking for us? I would have started looking for a way out of the building, but the property was surrounded by a high wall, and there was no back door. No other way out except through the front gate, with people firing guns all around us, and a helicopter spraying bullets on the community.

Ross, a former member of the U.S. Special Forces, found a large stick and positioned himself at the top of the stairs. He handed me a small propane tank.

"If any of the bad guys come up the steps, you throw that down on them," he said. It seems comical now, in hindsight, but in the moment we were doing what we thought we needed to do in order to protect ourselves and our friends.

I heard a voice downstairs, a man's frantic voice talking on the phone, asking lots of questions. Later I found out he was a worker there at the building, and he had called the Afghan government to try to find out what was going on. I could hear him talking on and on, and I wondered if he was getting any news or if help was on the way.

Eventually, as abruptly as it had started, the gunfire stopped. I looked at Ross. We weren't sure what to do. Soon the Afghan army was on the scene, escorting us out into the courtyard at gunpoint. I wouldn't say I felt threatened by their presence, but I definitely felt like the guns communicated this idea that I was supposed to stand exactly where they told me to stand until the situation was resolved. Their demeanor was appropriate but also intimidating.

Rubble was all around us. Glass was everywhere. Just down and across the street, where the bomb had gone off, massive security fences had crumbled. There was blood on the pavement. People were still wailing and crying out in loud voices. Ambulances lined the street. But Ross and I were given our freedom and told to leave the area.

A car came in and whisked us away. I sat very low in the back seat as we drove through the streets of Herat on our way to a safe house. By then everyone in the city knew what had happened, they knew the bombing had targeted Westerners (not us, but a different organization on the same street), and there we were, two American men being driven from one part of the city to another. People stared at us as the car flew by.

Later that day, when things had settled down and we had a chance to think clearly, Ross voiced the question I had been mulling over and over in my mind.

"So, do we stay or do we go?" Ross asked me once we had finally been positioned in a safe house.

At that moment I remembered one of our first interactions earlier in the week with the group of young Afghans. A Pashtun man had stood up to talk – Pashtuns are members of a very conservative tribe in Afghanistan. Their wives wear burkas and are completely covered except for their eyes. The men wear white, collared shirts with black vests and are usually very well groomed. It was one of these men who had stood up to speak.

"I have to tell you," he had said. "I think it's a mistake that you are here. I wish you were not here. I think you should leave our country."

Ross, undeterred, had engaged the man in conversation about why he felt that way. This was not the welcome we had hoped for upon our arrival in Herat.

I think you should leave our country.

In spite of the man's words, in those hours following the bombing, I didn't feel right about leaving. That Pashtun man was only one voice in that group of 20 or 30 students, and the others soaked up our presence, as if our being there validated the change they were trying to bring about. They were surrounded by influencers who told them they couldn't do it, who told them they could never bring change to Afghanistan. I felt like our voice of encouragement was sorely needed. Yet, I was justifiably nervous about staying and, if it had been easy to leave that day, I'm sure I would have taken that option.

"If we stay, where will we do the work?" I asked Ross, thinking of my own family at home. My wife and two children. Should I stay or should I go?

"I think there are other options where we can meet with the students," Ross said. "That's assuming, of course, that anyone shows up for the classes after what just happened."

I nodded. It was a difficult decision. By then we knew that we had not been the target, and most of the men responsible for the attack had been rounded up.

Ross led the effort to stay. He said, "It doesn't feel right to leave. Part of the work we're doing is showing these folks that you can get through this exact kind of power grab, that this old model of influence doesn't work. What does it say if we leave now?"

We were on the same page. We decided to stay for our remaining three days and do what we could. I don't remember any personal conversations with individual students during those last few days, at least not about the bombing, and the group did get a little smaller. Eighty percent of the students returned.

After a largely uneventful few days, we had a little celebration with the students on the last day. They brought in a potluck meal and I experienced, in a very sweet way, how different their culture was from ours. The men exhibited such physical intimacy toward each other – they sort of sprawled on the floor when they ate, resting and leaning against one another. It was a neat thing to see.

We left Herat as scheduled and headed back to Kabul. The bomb was big news, and everything in Kabul was tense. Everyone was on high alert. The city felt dark and angry.

On our way back to the airport, I found myself looking out the window at the houses, the same color as the surrounding mountains. I watched as this culture, different from mine, flashed past me. I had so many questions:

- What impact can I have on a community like this, where deep-seated traditions about power and culture seem to hold such influence?

- What could this trip have possibly accomplished?

- What impact can I really make?

- What impact can that classroom of individuals make surrounded by this kind of terror, intimidation, and corruption?

I thought about my business back in Texas and I realized millions of people in cubicles and offices across the United States are asking similar questions. Yes, they are in different circumstances but the core questions are the same. Everywhere in our country, people show up to work and perform tasks that, in their heart of hearts, they do not think are all that important. People in Dallas and St. Louis and Philadelphia are asking the same questions about influence and impact that people in Herat and Kabul are asking:

How can I make an impact? Me? How could someone like me have any influence in this company, in this world? I'm not powerful or prestigious, I'm just a (fill in the blank).

Wherever you find groups of people, you find hierarchies and chiefs and bosses. You find workers and slackers, nurturers and exploiters. And every single one of those individuals is trying to figure out how they fit in the community of people around them. It's a core longing, a primary desire, and it manifests itself in questions that all of us ask: Can I really make a difference? Can I have a positive influence on the lives of those around me?

Rollo May says in *Man's Search For Himself,* "The experience of emptiness...comes from people's feeling that they are powerless to do anything effective about their lives or the world they live in. Inner vacuousness is the long-term, accumulated result of a person's particular conviction toward himself (or herself), namely, that he cannot...effectually influence the world around him."

I watch my female colleagues face these questions in their own context. It is said of women today that they suffer from a confidence gap. I encounter female colleagues who wonder if they have what it takes to accomplish their career goals. Although women outnumber men in earned undergrad and graduate degrees and have filled the gap in middle management, they are still noticeably absent from the C-suite and make less than their male counterparts in similar roles.

For that reason, they can see the existing influence paradigm of Possessions, Pedigree, and Position and assume they have to be at a significant level of leadership, or come from the right background, or have received the right schooling, and possess the right resources to influence and impact the world around them.

But our world is full proof that this is not the case. Proof like Mary Barra, who started as an 18-year-old female co-op student from a blue-collar background and worked her way up to become the first female CEO of a major auto maker, General Motors. Proof like Ursula Burns, who began as a summer intern and worked her way through the ranks, even accepting a job as an executive assistant to the CEO knowing it offered uncommon exposure and experience, and ultimately became the first African American female CEO of a Fortune 500 company – Xerox. Something is happening, *something already has happened*, within our culture. Proof like Sara Blakely, who graduated from Florida State with a Communications degree and sold fax machines door to door while cultivating a hosiery idea. She overcame rejection and countless obstacles to become the founder of Spanx and one of the world's youngest self-made billionaires. In the corporate world, even for women, we're seeing the old model of influence being replaced by something new.

Regardless of whether you are a 23-year-old Afghan dreaming to one day make a difference or a woman in the U.S. in mid-level management feeling obscure, you need to understand something: It makes no difference if you're the CEO of a Fortune 500 company or a dressing room attendant at J.C. Penney. You have an enormous capacity to influence people.

If you feel empty, it may be because you feel powerless to effect change in your world. The good news for you is this: The influence paradigm is shifting.

LIFT

2
The Two Paradigms of Influence

LIFT

LIFT

The week prior to my time in Afghanistan, I spent a week in Kurdistan meeting with people in the Kurd government and discussing conflict resolution. While there, I visited the University of Duhok and spoke with the faculty. I led them in a discussion about the nature of change, and I loved the conversation. I got some very skeptical glances from the old school professors, as well as some very pointed questions. They weren't convinced by my assertions that the old structure of influence, one upheld by Possessions, Pedigree, and Position, was changing and needed to change. They weren't convinced by my belief that it was no longer sufficient for only those with the right amount of Possessions, the right Pedigree and the right Position to influence the landscape of their world. They simply couldn't envision it any other way. They couldn't imagine that any other model could be productive or work in the long term.

A young man approached me afterwards and tried to explain the situation. He had done his undergraduate work in the U.S. and had a good sense of the difference in our respective cultures.

"The older faculty want to hold on to how things have been. This is the system they have been trained under, a system they have sacrificed for. They want to maintain control strictly because they are old and experienced, not because of what they have to offer."

"But what about you?" I asked. "What do you want?"

He shrugged.

"We don't want it to be like that anymore."

He wasn't alone. One of the few women who came to our leadership development program in Afghanistan was a medical doctor. She was a sharp thinker and I could tell she was soaking up everything that was said, every new idea that was presented. I was impressed she was even there, and I wondered about her background, what her family thought about her being there, and what her dreams and aspirations were.

The thing is, because of the way influence currently works in Afghanistan, she couldn't participate in the same way as the men. Our evening sessions were attended by a much more conservative group than our daytime sessions, so at night she sat off to the side of the group, as if she was reassuring the men there that she knew she didn't belong. She never spoke unless she was very specifically asked a question. She wouldn't get in the group pictures that we took – the more conservative elements of that culture view it as improper for women to be in photographs.

I saw her shortly after the bomb went off and she was in tears. I can't help but wonder if, along with being saddened by the destruction and death, her tears didn't also flow because of what the bomb represented: a violent effort to maintain the old paradigm of influence. Was that explosion a desperate attempt to maintain the deeply ingrained power structures, the very structures that kept her at arms length? I have to believe she mourned the continuation of a paradigm that would suppress her daughters and her nieces and, if not stopped, someday even her granddaughters.

Prior to the bomb, though, I could feel a sense of hope building among the young men and women attending our classes; a hope that things could change and their country could be a better place. Our very presence seemed to encourage them. Maybe the rest of the world did care about what was happening there. Maybe the rest of the world did want to see them succeed.

But the bomb seemed to put things in check. It represented a group of people who would do anything to ensure that the status quo remained. The bomb represented a group of people who would do anything to keep that young woman, along with everyone else in the country, trapped in the old model of influence.

I call it "Static Influence."

Afghanistan is the perfect example of a place torn between the old and new models of influence. Afghans recently finished an election that had a phenomenal turnout despite the threats and bombs, despite the Taliban telling people that if they vote, they will be harmed. Even at great danger to themselves, large numbers of Afghan people are voting.

But the old influence paradigm, Static Influence, is still easily spotted.

What are the foundations of Static Influence?

Possessions, Pedigree, and Position.

The central tenant of Static Influence is the idea that those in power are the only influencers, and power itself is determined by those people who have Possessions, Pedigree, and Position.

Possessions (and therefore influence) throughout time have only been in the hands of the wealthiest individuals. Those with resources could grow the most food, hire the most mercenaries, and control the largest pieces of land. The rich had the Possessions, and they pushed their influence on everyone around them.

This is still true all over the world. In Africa, those who control the roads needed for transporting materials and supplies have Possessions. In the Middle East, those with control of the oil and gas reserve have Possessions. Those in Possessions-based influence positions often feel threatened by "subordinates" who come up with good ideas or show promising signs of leadership. Those at the head of the pack rarely pull back and let someone else take over the lead position for a time. Those at the front either find the ideas of those at the back inferior . . . or they steal their ideas without giving them credit.

While Possessions was one of the original determiners of influence, at some point very early on it split and another branch was formed: Pedigree. As history progressed, the Possessions-based influencers decided that they wanted their children to take the reins after they were gone. Influence became an inheritance, and the only way you could influence was if you were born into a certain Position. Think pharaohs, ancient kings, or many of the tyrannical despots around the world today.

We see this at work in the power structures that lead some Middle Eastern countries, places like the United Arab Emirates or Saudi Arabia, where the only ones who wield influence are those who were born into families that already hold positions based on Possessions. If you don't have the right Pedigree, then you don't have any say in what goes on or how things are done.

No doubt, those powerful families exist in every modern culture. Certainly families like the Rockefellers, Kennedys and, more recently, the Bushes and Clintons, have helped shape the country we live in, and if you are privileged to share their lineage you still can trade successfully on the family name. Additionally, there are also well-run family businesses where having the same last name as the company founder will gain you extra access and more latitude.

But most of us in the United States would scoff at the old influence paradigm. Most of us don't take people seriously when they've been given influence simply because of who their parents are or what kind of background they come from. Most of us wouldn't allow someone to influence our lives just because they are bigger or stronger than we are.

Yet there's a third manifestation of the old influence paradigm that is deeply rooted even in western culture. It's one of the main culprits that keeps individuals from influencing, and too many organizations are bogged down in the type of Static Influence it introduces.

What I'm talking about is Position.

Whenever someone "pulls rank" as a last resort to maintain his hold on a group; whenever someone vetoes a perfectly good idea because it wasn't hers; whenever someone is excluded from a group because of his title (or lack thereof): this is Static Influence rearing its ugly head.

Now, I'm not someone who argues that positions and hierarchies within organizations should be eliminated. Organizational structure can be helpful. Teams need leaders. If no one knows who is responsible, then no one is responsible.

But when Position determines someone's ability (or inability) to influence others in an organization, then that organization is firmly rooted in the old paradigm. It is almost a guarantee that only the big, strong men are influencing or that leadership positions are limited to the children of the founder. It doesn't matter which part of the old paradigm you're practicing – Possessions, Pedigree, or Position. When followed blindly, they all dehumanize people by eliminating their ability to influence.

Why is it so important to recognize how the old influence paradigm is showing up in your organization? Because a new kind of influence is growing in power.

Moisés Naím in *The End of Power* talks about the shift happening in influence. Two examples he gives might help illustrate the shift more clearly.

First, he talks about how the wealthy are losing their influence of Possessions because of the dramatic economic changes that have taken place. When the tech bubble burst in 2001 and the mortgage bubble in 2008, some influential people lost their influence because, quite practically, they lost their Possession power. I know what you're thinking: "But the wealthy are wealthier than ever before! The gap between the haves and the have-nots is wider than it has ever been!" Naím would agree that income is concentrating, and some are using this concentration of Possessions to gain political power. But in Naím's opinion, that consolidation, while both troublesome and unacceptable, doesn't signify stability for those holding Possessions. In fact, those in the top one percent of income have experienced even more instability than the rest of society! Naím quotes Emmanual Saez, a Berkeley economics professor, who notes:

The recent Great Recession caused a 36.3 percent drop in the incomes of the top one percent of earners in the United States, compared to an 11.6 percent drop for the remaining 99 percent. Steven Kaplan at the University of Chicago's Booth School of Business has calculated that the proportion of income accounted for by the top one percent fell from its peak of 23.5 percent of income in 2007 to 17.6 percent in 2009 and it kept falling in following years.

Think of the companies that were one time visible and influential companies that have disappeared from the public eye or have lost public approval because of the Great Recession: AIG, Goldman Sachs and Lehman Brothers. Even Possessions, once a pillar of Static Influence, is less stable than it has ever been before, and those at the top are losing more than they ever have, opening the way for people who don't have a wealth of possessions to earn a voice that has not been able to be heard until now.

Second, Naím talks about this changing nature of power becoming evident in the way that the military power of nations is losing its influence. Naím sites a Harvard study that notes in recent wars that the weaker side has prevailed more often than the militarily stronger side. Think about the victories ISIS is currently having against major military powers throughout the world. Think about the war in Vietnam. Think about the Revolutionary War and the victory the colonists won against the great British Army. If the "weaker" side is prevailing in battle, then I have to wonder if the same wouldn't be true of "weaker" businesses or "weaker" organizations. Influence is shifting into the hands of the less likely, the smaller.

There are many reasons for this shift. First, the current state of influence emerged from structures that kept those in power from encountering those who would unseat them. These artificial barriers, like rules that govern elections, weapons, police forces, proprietary technology, and even personal charisma or religious authority, limited competition and created a cycle of ever-growing power for those in the seat of influence.

These barriers that shielded incumbents from rivals have weakened in the last 30 years. Because of political and economic changes, access to markets through transportation and technology, the influence of media and social media, people can now, more easily than ever, get past these barriers.

If you look at the sociological history and dig into the question of who gets to lead and who doesn't, it's actually a fairly recent phenomenon that individuals not born to the right family, gender, race, geographic location or sexual orientation now have a greater opportunity to influence.

Think about that for a second.

The barriers are coming down.

By virtue of access to information, your own availability, and availability of resources, individuals have more choices and ways of influencing than ever before. You can write a blog that's accessible to anyone in the world. You can self-publish a book or record your own album. You can start a business and immediately have customers all around the globe. You have direct access to things like the stock market, the commodities markets, and websites like Wikipedia that will give you any piece of information you need, at any given moment.

An even more recent phenomenon is that you can do all of this from your cell phone.

This ability to influence is unprecedented in human history. You don't have to be big to accomplish big things. You don't have to be a huge organization to have huge influence.

This new order in the world is shedding the old paradigm of Static Influence based around Position, Possessions, and Pedigree. A new paradigm of influence is coming into the world, a paradigm based around Community, Character, and Choice.

I call this "Dynamic Influence."

From the fall of the Berlin Wall to the modern day Arab Spring, the last 30 years have seen this massive process of evolving structures. And when the nature of "who holds the power" changes, so, too, does the nature of influence.

You don't have to look any farther than social media to understand the power that community has in creating influence. From crowdfunding and Kickstarter campaigns, to products going viral (songs, books, videos, ideas) and government leadership being ousted (the Arab Spring), we are learning that those who can best leverage their networks are the ones making waves.

Community is critical in Dynamic Influence because our community has always been the context in which we influence and in many cases can be the engine behind our influence. Within our reach in any given context are people who have either the knowledge and/or experience we lack or a connection to people we don't yet know. They have the maps to places we want to go and access to the people we want to see. But community, as we will see, is not just something we take from, it's something we must contribute to. For if we can see and meet the needs of our community, we can gain the credibility and trust needed to access their help when the time comes.

Character is also critical in Dynamic Influence because our best leadership comes out of who we are and what we know. Researchers confirm it's not in shoring up our weaknesses but rather by leaning into our strengths that we are most effective. People who understand their talents and skills and find ways to strengthen them and then use them to contribute value become influential. Think of the people you seek advice and help from in your life. I would wager they are most likely seasoned veterans in the area you're asking their counsel, schooled by experience. They are people who put in the time to know what they are talking about and be good at their craft. Competency is a core component of Character. But beyond competency, character is enhanced by compassion. When you think of the people who you credit most with influencing your life (coaches, teachers, bosses, mentors), they often aren't just people who you trusted to be competent, they are also people who are compassionate. Aren't they the ones who believed in you, affirmed a hidden talent in you, pushed you to become all you could be? They are people who "saw you" and used their expertise and experience for your good. In our world we gain greater influence when we are not just good at what we do but when we earn trust and favor from people we influence through compassion. It's the old adage: "People don't care how much you know until they know how much you care."

Then there is Choice, the third foundation of Dynamic Influence. The difference between knowing and doing is choosing. So often people understand, in theory, their capacity to influence but it is a select few who choose to do something about it. It is people who fight through fear and apathy who change the landscape around them. Women like Mary Barra and Ursula Burns who rose to positions of influence by choosing to engage the challenges in front of them, learn, and find a way to add value. This is the power of choice.

One of my favorite recent examples of Character, Community and Choice is the story of Sugata Mitra and his "Hole In The Wall" experiment.

Mitra, an Indian professor of Education Technology at Newcastle University in England, had the bold idea that kids in Indian slums with little to no formal education had the capacity to teach themselves the same material other children were learning from teachers. Mitra chose to put his idea to the test. He put a computer in the wall of a New Delhi slum and discovered it took children, who had never seen a computer before, only hours to teach themselves to browse the Internet and record their own music. A later experiment proved a group of English-speaking Indian children with indiscernible English accents could teach themselves to adapt their accents to be recognized by a speech-to-text program in two months. A final group of students managed to teach themselves biotechnology simply by being given the computer resources necessary and the challenge.

Mitra's pedagogical method was simple. When he presented a problem to students and they inquired, "How will we do this?" he responded simply with, "I have no idea." He gave them the freedom to search and discover the solution for themselves and find a way that worked. Mitra asserts in our ever-adapting world, the future leaders will not be subject matter experts, but relentless explorers and hunter-gatherers. They will be the problem solvers, the people who are willing to enter into the challenges we face and find a way to find a way.

Mitra believed in the capacity of these children. He believed, when faced with a problem, a little compassionate challenge could inspire them to choose to overcome fear, engage, and find a solution (Choice). He found in his experiment, much of the children's success was due to their collaboration. They pushed and helped one another achieve their shared goal (Community). And their collective desire to grow enabled them not only to gain understanding and skill (Character) but also to achieve far more than anyone expected. In the process these kids, and Mitra, surprised the world. Today Mitra's experiment has been replicated all over the world and has challenged the way we are seeing education.

This dynamic form of influence is all over our world if we have eyes to see it. And it is within our reach if we have the courage to go after it.

So what happens when you use Dynamic Influence in the heart

of an American city that's been running on Static Influence for nearly two centuries?

Enter Dallas real estate developer Scott Rohrman and the story of how he's putting Dynamic Influence to work in one of Dallas' most troubled areas.

LIFT

3
Rescuing Deep Ellum

LIFT

It was nearly 9 p.m. when I took the exit to downtown Dallas and headed east a few blocks. The side road I was on traced the overpass and that feeling of uncertainty overcame me as I drove through the deep shadows of the night. I left the comfort of freeway behind and drove into the city.

I passed a large, neon sign that announced I had arrived in "Deep Ellum."

Originally called Deep Elm, Deep Ellum had, through the years, been quite the place. Live music had sprung up there, fostered by dozens of nightclubs and restaurants. Weekend festivals sometimes left the streets in that part of Dallas undriveable. People flocked to Deep Ellum for its lively nightlife and tangible sense of hope.

But when I drove into Deep Ellum in the spring of 2014, it was mostly just a continuation of the shadows I had found under the overpass. Derelict buildings, empty alleyways, darkened streetlights…this is what the years had done to Deep Ellum.

I pulled my car into a small parking space in front of a glass storefront, one of the only buildings on that block with the lights still on. I got out and walked up to the door and knocked on the glass. I looked at my watch, then peered into the building. It didn't look like anyone was there. I knocked again. A thin young man with long hair pulled into a ponytail came down the stairs and opened the door.

"You must be Tom," he said, smiling.

"That's right," I said, shaking his hand.

"Scott should be here any minute. Come on in and have a seat."

Scott is an old friend of mine, someone who is using the new paradigm of influence to resurrect Deep Ellum. When Scott entered the room and started talking, I couldn't help but be blown

away by how he is using Dynamic Influence in his attempts to reju-
venate Deep Ellum. This was remarkable to me because Deep Ellum – and Dallas as a whole – is a city that has been mired in Static
Influence since its inception. Possessions, Pedigree, and Position
have determined the direction of Dallas for the last 170 years.

Dallas and Fort Worth are two cities made great by families like
the Perots who transformed the technology information industry, the Murchisons, Hunts and Hills who changed the oil industry
and have contributed to both business development and cultural
development in Dallas, the Crows who expanded real estate, the
Minyard family who shaped the food industry, the Bass family who
helped build Fort Worth into what it is today, and the Carpenters
who are building Las Colinas.

All of these families and their descendants are still influential
in Dallas today because of who they are and what their families
have done to shape the city. And, rightly so. But the beautiful thing
about Dallas is you don't have to be part of these families to have
influence. All over Dallas we are seeing a new breed of influencers raise up to shape our city. Catalytic entrepreneurs, young professionals with a will to contribute, and activists passionate about
policy, most of whom don't have the pedigree these families do.
They are bringing ingenuity and ideas to the marketplace that are
not only gaining attention but are earning them a voice.

We are seeing Dynamic Influence gaining ground. Scott Rohrman is the perfect example. Scott is a middle-class preacher's kid
from Mississippi who became a real estate developer. He doesn't
have any fancy pedigree, and he didn't come from a position of
power. He simply worked hard and developed his business to the
point where he could seize the opportunity in front of him. And
he is in the process of changing Dallas.

"I had a guy call me today," Scott said, motioning for me to sit
down in a small arm chair. "He's connected with a private, mem-
bers-only club that wants to open a branch in Deep Ellum. He

wanted to come down and check out the community, and he wanted me to tell him which building he should look at."

Scott kind of laughed and then looked at me. When he realized I wasn't getting the punch line, he pressed forward.

"I told him, look, I'm not going to tell you which building. I'm not going to tell you how much I'm charging for rent. I'm not going to tell you anything until you come down here and meet and then I'll tell you about my kids and you can tell me about your kids and we'll walk around Deep Ellum together so that you can understand my vision. I'll ask you what you like about running a club, what your passion is, what drives you in life."

He paused, pushing his finger into the arm of his chair to emphasize his point.

"Then we'll decide if there's a fit. We're building a community here, and I need to find out if they want to be part of this community. That's way more important to me than how much rent they'll pay."

What did the club owner say?

"He said, 'I've never heard anything like this. So you're doing this like it's an art? You're taking the artist approach instead of the financial approach?' That's about right. I tell everyone the same thing: I bought 27 buildings in Deep Ellum, and I'm going to turn it into a blank canvas, and then I want to find good people who bring good concepts who, in turn, will bring good customers to paint on that blank canvas. To help build a community."

He shrugged his shoulders.

"That's all we're trying to do here. Build a good community."

There were a lot of things about Deep Ellum that Scott wanted to improve when he started the project, and because he owned so many of the buildings, he could have gone in with a heavy hand

and made most of the changes he wanted to make. He could have used two of the foundations of Static Influence to get his way: Possessions and Position. But that wasn't the kind of community he wanted to create. He wanted a community where people worked together, where people influenced each other, a community where everyone felt like they had a say in the work of art that was being created.

One of the challenges Scott encountered early on had to do with graffiti. Because there were so many vacant buildings and abandoned lots, graffiti artists had set up camp. There was one parking lot in particular that was centralized in Deep Ellum, a lot that he wanted to clean up and get some bright lights on. It had a large expanse of walls on three sides, and it tended to be a magnet for graffiti.

In the old model of influence, someone in Scott's position would have put up security cameras and notified the police to make extra rounds to keep the graffiti artists away. If that failed, he would have hired private security to patrol the area, eventually landing some kids in jail and increasing the tension in the neighborhood. The old model of influence would have protected that area at all costs because keeping clean walls would have become a symbol for who held the power in that community.

But Scott doesn't work that way.

Instead he called all the graffiti artists in the neighborhood together and paid them to create an amazing mural all along the walls. Once it was up, none of the other graffiti artists would paint over it – that's a point of honor within their system, not painting over each other's work. Finally, Scott plans to institute an annual contest open to graffiti artists, inviting them to come to that particular parking lot and paint on one of the walls. The neighborhood would get to vote on which of the three they like best. If anyone wins three years in a row, then their art would stay permanently.

Talk about engaging a community instead of alienating it! Talk about discarding the old ways of influence and trading them in for something much more effective and beautiful!

This is a perfect illustration of the three foundational elements of Dynamic Influence: Community, Character, and Choice. He's engaging the community and encouraging them to determine the kind of community they want to create. He's respecting the individual character of those who live there and setting them up for a win instead of creating a community where their character will be easily undermined. And he's providing an element of choice for those who are involved, empowering them to turn around and influence each other.

Community, Character, and Choice.

Dynamic Influence is transforming Deep Ellum.

Scott walked into a bar in Deep Ellum. He had been hearing for a few months how the owner of that particular establishment had been saying a lot of bad stuff about him behind his back, warning the rest of Deep Ellum that Scott was only there to raise their rents or kick them out. Since this guy had been a member of the community for a long time and was an influential voice, people listened to him. Scott decided he was going to talk to this guy face-to-face.

Scott is a fairly standard businessman, at least in the way he presents himself, so he walked into this bar with his dress slacks, nice shoes, and a button-down shirt. He saw the owner (we'll call him Bob) standing behind the bar, doing some cleaning, probably getting ready for the evening business. Bob wore jeans, a sleeveless shirt, and his arms were covered in tattoos from his wrists to his shoulders.

Scott approached him directly. There's no beating around the bush where he's concerned.

LIFT

"Hi, I'm Scott."

Bob looked up and immediately frowned.

"I know who you are."

"I hear you have some concerns about the direction of Deep Ellum," Scott said. "Let's talk."

"I don't have time to talk," Bob said. "I've got to do inventory. I've got to clean up. I don't have time to talk to you."

Scott stared at him for a minute.

"Okay, well, keep this in mind. The next time you decide to talk about me behind my back, you just remember that I came down here and tried to talk to you face-to-face."

Scott turned around and walked toward the exit. Just before he put his hand out to push open the door, Bob shouted behind him.

"Why would I want to talk to the asshole who's going to come in here and raise all of our rents?"

Scott turned around.

"That's a start," Scott said. "At least now you're talking to my face."

The two men got into a long discussion about Deep Ellum. Scott shared his vision for the neighborhood. He could see Bob softening.

"But you're just going to raise our rent," Bob insisted again.

"Listen, do you think your business would go up if all of these buildings around here had businesses in them and the streets were well lit and we had concerts coming in here in the evenings?"

"Well, yeah," Bob said begrudgingly.

"Let's say this whole thing really takes off and there are people on these streets every night of the week and all day, too," Scott said, his eyes lighting up with excitement at the prospect of a revitalized Deep Ellum "Don't you think you'd do a lot more business?"

"Well, yeah," Bob admitted.

"If your business doubled, would you mind paying a couple hundred dollars more rent every month?"

"I guess not."

"That's all I'm trying to do here. I'm trying to make things better for everyone. I'm trying to bring back the old Deep Ellum, the Deep Ellum that was packed on weekend nights, the Deep Ellum that was humming with people and excitement and a sense that this is a special community."

How do you get a man in slacks and a button-down shirt to partner effectively with a man who has tattoo sleeves?

You start to work within these elements of Dynamic Influence. You start to rely on Community, Character, and Choice to influence people.

Using Dynamic Influence means not avoiding the difficult conversations – even with critics, it means facing them head on.

Using Dynamic Influence means valuing everyone, even those who are different, and seeking out opinions and ways of thinking unlike your own.

Dynamic Influence doesn't plow over people just because you have the contracts in place to do so. It takes time to help others understand your perspective with humility and an open mind.

If Dynamic Influence can change a place like Deep Ellum, it can work anywhere. Even in your community.

LIFT

4
Define Your Tribe

LIFT

If we've learned anything so far, it's that the barriers are breaking down and our communities are more open than ever before to the new model of Dynamic Influence. Because you no longer require Possessions, Pedigree, or Position in order to influence your community, anyone can influence. And this is important, because if we feel powerless to influence those around us, we feel empty. Fortunately, Dynamic Influence is enabling more and more people to influence. Whether you're designated as a leader or not, you can influence. Whether you sit in a traditional seat of power or not, you can influence.

You can influence from the front of the pack, and you can also influence from the back.

When the guys in my bike-riding groups see buzzards circling, they know it's time to come back and rescue me. You see, this is a group I've been riding with, they're all faster than me. I say it's because they're all younger than I am, but we all have excuses, don't we?

The truth is, they're all better at bike riding. The other (fortunate) truth is, they're just really nice guys.

I stay with the pack for as long as I can, and they adjust the group so someone different is always leading and someone else is always at the back with me, drafting for me, keeping me company, making sure I don't drift too far back and lose the advantage of staying with the group. Any rider that becomes isolated quickly falls far behind and loses any hope of catching up to the fast-moving riders. I didn't ask them, they just started coming back, picking me up, keeping me in the pack.

The funniest thing started to happen. As they've come back, one by one, I've started to learn about their lives, their journeys. And maybe because I am a bit older, have older kids, am a little farther along in life, some of the guys started asking for my advice, running things by me and asking what I thought. As the years passed, I would learn that those talks had been meaningful to them. They found value in what I had to say, even though I was at the back of the pack.

Do you look at those around you and envy their positions of leadership? Do you wish you had what it took to always ride at the front? Do you sometimes battle feelings of worthlessness when you're lagging behind everyone else?

Take heart.

Because of this new world of Dynamic Influence, even those who ride at the back of the pack can make a difference.

One of these guys I got to know during a back-of-the-pack season ended up coming to work with me at Symbolist. One Monday at the office, we had a conversation. He was telling me about life in the neighborhood where he lived and mentioned that his family had just been invited to their neighbor's house.

"That's cool," I said.

"Yeah," he said, pausing. "I don't think we'll go."

"Really? Why not?"

"We're different from them," he said. "Our kids don't really get along with their kids. It just doesn't seem like a good fit."

I sensed an opportunity to challenge him in a way that would expand his community, enlarge his life.

"It's only one night," I said. "What if you showed up intentionally, coached your kids beforehand and used it as a way to grow as a family? What if you said, hey, let's go be friendly for one night?"

"Thanks for sharing that," he said thoughtfully. "I'll definitely consider it."

The next Monday, he came straight over to me.

"Tom," he said, "I thought through what you said last Monday and decided we should go . . . we had so much fun, and we definitely made new friends."

So many times we miss opportunities because we don't seize the circumstances right in front of us. Yes, that night could have been uncomfortable for my friend and his family — we've all been there. But it wasn't. Plus, he got a chance to show his kids what can happen when you make the most of an opportunity right in front of you.

What humbled me most was realizing I had a chance to help my friend learn to exert his own influence. I got that chance because of those conversations on our bike rides when he came to the back and rode with me.

What if I had a terrible attitude about being at the back of the pack? What if I was so determined NOT to be at the back of the pack that I spent every minute on the bike stewing and complaining and being angry? What if I thought all those guys at the front were doing it on purpose, leaving me behind just to make me feel bad?

I would have lost a big opportunity to influence good men. Having a bad attitude about being at the back of the pack will stifle your ability to influence; in fact, continuing to have a bad attitude eventually will separate you completely from the group (whether in biking or in work or at home). Soon enough, you'll find yourself completely alone.

Fortunately for me, I had been willing to accept my position in that particular group.

You can influence your community from wherever you are, leader or follower, front of the pack or back of the pack. But this realization, while important, naturally raises another very important question, a question that you may never have considered.

Who is your pack?

Think about that for a minute. Who is your community? Who are the people you rub shoulders with on a regular basis? Who do you live with, work with, play with? What is your role in each of these different spheres? What do people depend on you for, and what do you depend on others for?

That question is important because the people you keep time with give you a sense of who you are and why your contribution is valuable. They are also the context within which you can be the most influential. If you care for them well, they can be the horsepower behind your ability to influence at greater levels.

The interesting thing about communities is they, too, are changing. The kinds of communities we have today are vastly different from the kinds of communities people had 40 years ago, or even 10 years ago. In fact, if someone from *that* era would look at people in *this* era, they would have questions of their own.

They would probably ask, *"Where has community gone?"*

Many of the traditional communities have evaporated. Families aren't as cohesive as they used to be, fractured by high rates of divorce and the relatively normal practice of following a job across the country. Millennials especially are less rooted to a physical location than any preceding generation, and with the unpredictable nature of our current economy and the relative ease of long-distance transportation, they are more open to following a job wherever it might lead them. Baby Boomers are retiring and heading south. Gen Xers, left behind by their retiring parents and younger friends, are exploring the idea of relocating. I run into fewer and fewer people these days who can say, "I grew up here."

Church provided a sense of community for centuries, but it seems to be less and less a part of most people's lives today.

There's a growing disconnect between the present generation and organized religion. (I have a feeling it has to do with religion's continued reliance on Static Influence, but I don't have any evidence to back that up.) Even long-standing community organizations, like the Lion's Club, Rotary and VFW, seem to be unable to engage younger generations, and their buildings are going into disrepair.

We've become less connected with those who live next door to us. In the 50s and 60s, when today's suburbs were being built, it seemed to herald a new level of community. People were no longer living on farms – they were living close together. They parked on the street and saw their neighbors every morning and every afternoon.

But with the move to the suburbs, we also became more dependent on our vehicles. We started driving to our homes through back alleys to park in garages, and our neighbors never saw our faces. Work hours increased. All of these things led to a highly individualized society where we depend less on our neighbors and have less influence on those in our neighborhoods.

And now, even when we do go outside, most of us are looking at a screen of some kind. It is easy to see this behavior as people are becoming more and more estranged from the community right in front of them.

As I talked through this phenomenon of technology infiltrating every aspect of our lives with the young professionals in my company, they pointed out to me that our overuse of phones isn't necessarily a forsaking of the community in front of us as much as it is our new way of seeking out community. We feel the desire for community – to be known – but in a world that has made connection difficult, we search for community wherever we might be able to find it – even if that's on Facebook or Twitter or Pinterest.

So, where *are* we finding community?

How are we finding our pack?

The answer might surprise you.

Work has become one of the primary places we're finding community. For most of us, we spend the vast majority of our time and lives at work. It is where we use our skills and experience to add value. As a happy result, it also becomes our place to connect and engage in purpose with others. Think about how some of the well-known organizations like Google or Apple design their work areas, creating events and spaces where small groups of people gravitate and interact. Instead of simply creating a place where people get work done and leave, these companies are creating environments where people feel comfortable to live and work to the fullest. But it's not just at work that we are finding our communities.

We're also finding community where we exercise and where we play. Organizations like CrossFit are maximizing fitness in community and garnering millions of followers as a result. We're still finding our communities where we worship. Some of us have started to revisit the idea of what it means to be a good neighbor, and we're beginning to build community in new, unique ways.

Regardless of where you find your community, it is of utmost importance that you find it. And when you find your pack or your tribe, you've found your place to make a difference. But to truly make a difference you will need to know the needs of the people in your community.

One of my friends often speaks to large groups in her free time. She knows from years of training that before she ever gets up on stage, before she even starts her manuscript, she must first ask: Who is my audience? What are their needs, desires, and fears? Where am I trying to take them and do they want to go there with me? How is what I'm going to say helpful to them? How can I use what I have to help them get to where they need to go?

This idea of identifying and understanding your audience or your community is critical if we ever want to be influential.

Recently, at a Fortune 500 company, our company led a group of female leaders through a workshop discussing how to increase their influence at work. All of these women are intelligent, highly motivated and capable, and they are all looking to increase their influence inside the company specifically with their company leaders.

We started the session by asking them, "Who influences you and why"? Examples came of men and women who are famous, who have great ideas, who are powerful, but also of normal people who have cared for them, inspired them, challenged and helped them in some important way.

Then we asked them to list for themselves the people in the company they would like to influence and asked, "If you are influenced in these ways, don't you think those people you are trying to influence are, too?" Of course they are. The question is how can we influence these people in those ways?

To answer that question, consider this exercise called "Get Up On the Balcony" made famous by Ronald Heifetz, a Harvard Professor:

"Imagine walking into a ballroom for a fancy dinner party. The ballroom floor is expansive but relatively empty when you first arrive. As the guests begin to trickle in, things become more and more packed. Conversations get louder. Waiters and waitresses weave their way in among the partygoers. Someone drops a glass and it shatters on the floor, the contents spilling in every direction. It's chaotic.

Before the chaos, you were talking to one person and then they walked off so you began talking to someone else. Soon you're in a large group, a semi-circle of people, all talking at once. You try to get to the food table but everyone is shoulder to shoulder.

If someone walked up to you in that moment and asked you to describe the room, it would be pretty difficult. You're surrounded by people and commotion. You can barely move, let alone get a good glimpse of the entire floor.

But imagine that same person asks you to follow them. They weave their way through the room to broad staircase leading you to an upper level balcony where you can look down on the party.

You can see things much more clearly from there. You can see the various groups of people scattered throughout the room, the small cliques huddled around each other, the loners making their way along the edge of the wall. You can even see a pattern in the way the waitstaff walks around.

Now if you were asked to describe the party could you? Of course you could. Sometimes you just need to elevate your perspective to gain a better picture of what's happening."

Often, when people are considering how to increase their influence and impact they are only focused on their goal. But if we want to be influential with people, we need to get an elevated view and ask the question, "What are the goals of the people I'm trying to influence and how can I help them?"

We asked the women in our session to pick one person on their list and consider:

1. What is that person trying to accomplish in the organization?

2. What do I bring to the table that can help them succeed?

3. How can I practically offer my help?

So, what does it look like for a company to be influential with its people?

Well, let's take Chili's for example. One of my favorite companies to engage with is Brinker International, which owns the Chili's brand. "Chiliheads," as the employees are called, are a tight-knit, lively crew of great people. Walk onto the Brinker campus at any given moment and you may find them in a costume contest around Halloween, enjoying a chili cook-off on the grounds or engaged in some kind of work with St. Jude's, the charity they have embraced and, by the way, contributed more than 50 million dollars to as a company.

Experts say that right now in our country there is a War On Talent. The marketplace is open for good people to go where they really want. And for that reason, Brinker, like everyone else, is trying to hire and retain great people. And how they are doing it is by seeking to meet the needs of their employees.

If you follow Brinker's Twitter feed or "like" them on Facebook you'd realize they unmistakably care about their people. But this year, they did something extraordinary. They turned their yearly leadership retreat into "A Purpose Experience." Like most organizations, they used to spend 80 percent of that retreat talking about business and 20 percent investing in their people. This year, they flipped it. They spent the majority of their time investing in their people's well-being. Inspired by Rath and Harter's book *Well Being*, they offered five different tracks of learning focused on the five core areas of human well-being: career, social, financial, physical, and community. They brought in financial planners and fitness coaches. They inspired one another, shared their dreams with one another, and committed to help each other achieve their goals. The tagline they gave this "Experience" was: "Best you, best us, best life," because Brinker's leadership truly believes that if they want to succeed as a business they must help their employees succeed as people. The best possible version of their company is only possible when their people are at their best.

And as a result, the people at Brinker increasingly love where they work. Just check out #chilislove and you'll see.

- Who are your people?

- Who do you live with, work with, and play with?

- Who's your tribe, your pack?

That's your community.

Now, get up on the balcony.

- What does your community need?

- What are they trying to accomplish?

- What do you bring to the table that can help?

- How can you use what you have to help them?

If you never take the time to assess your community and figure out what role you have to play and how you can add value, the community loses out because your role goes unfilled and your value is never heard or experienced. Which means you – and they – lose out. Because we were all designed to influence – and, the good news is, we can.

LIFT

LIFT

5
Healthy Communities Require Healthy Environments

LIFT

LIFT

As I flew away from the Middle East, I have to admit, I felt a sense of relief. The day I put my hand on the refrigerator handle and the bomb went off outside the apartment, I wondered if I would make it out alive. I wondered if I would ever see my family again. When I stood with that small group of people on the second floor, planning our defense of the building, I thought my time on Earth might be up. So as the plane rose out of Kabul, and that dark valley receded behind me, a huge weight lifted.

But I also was cognizant of those I left, wonderful young people with big dreams who couldn't simply get on a plane and fly away from their troubles. I had a twinge of survivor's guilt, even though we stayed after the bombing and continued the work. I wondered what would become of those business people, students, and community members who so desperately wanted change.

At the core of us, we all ask, "Can I really have a positive influence on the lives of those around me?" Sometimes it's hard to believe that. But once we accept that everyone can make a difference, another big question confronts us, and it's one that I faced as I flew out of Afghanistan. It called everything I was teaching into question. It challenged the core of everything I was beginning to believe about influence.

"Can Dynamic Influence, the kind where everyone makes a difference, really work everywhere?"

That's the real question, isn't it? I mean, maybe this new model is gaining ground in the west, where people are relatively free and businesses aren't as regulated, where leaders seem to want what's best for people and violence is at an all-time low. But can it work in places like Afghanistan, where violence seems to be an everyday occurrence? Can Dynamic Influence work in Kurdistan, where the old model of influence is so deeply entrenched?

Can it work in your office, where your boss rules with an iron fist?

Can it work in your home, fractured by disagreements and hurt?

Can Dynamic Influence work everywhere?

A few days after I got home from the trip, I began scrolling through photos I had taken in Kurdistan. One of the photos was of a group of cyclists riding the city streets. I tend to notice cyclists wherever I go, but I took a picture of these Kurdistan riders because I was shocked by how much they looked like the guys I ride with in the States. People use bikes for transportation all over the world, but you don't see guys in Lycra riding high-end racing bikes just anywhere.

As I looked at the photo, something jumped out at me for the first time: the background. It was clearly new construction. I remembered seeing it all over Erbil. So what was so significant to me about a photo of Lycra-clad riders riding high-end bikes past new construction in Northern Iraq?

This:

When safety is assured and relative prosperity is in place, that environment enables people to flourish.

I realized Dynamic Influence doesn't just happen on its own when you understand your community, its needs, and the role you play. Dynamic Influence happens when you cultivate the right environment for influence and growth to take place.

Well, how do you do that? Good question. To explain, we're going to use the analogy of building an actual office throughout the rest of this chapter to describe what is needed to build a healthy work environment for influence.

Just as in building an office you must first get the foundation right, so, too, in building a healthy environment, the foundation must be solid for influence to have firm footing.

LIFT

Step 1. Make sure your foundation is solid

When I decided to build the Symbolist building, one of the first things I had to do was test and treat the soil. That may sound silly to someone who hasn't built before, but in Grapevine, Texas where our company is located, the soil is most commonly clay. It expands and contracts based on the amount of moisture in the ground, and as you can imagine that does a number on foundations. For that reason, I had to have an Olympic-size swimming pool hole dug on our property and have the soil treated with components that made the soil stable enough for a foundation. This was not an inexpensive endeavor but it was critical for ensuring the stability and strength of our building over the long haul.

One thing that can destroy a good company's foundation is fear. When an environment is laden with fear, and until you either eliminate that fear or support it with stronger components, there's not a lot you can do to help people fully engage. Think about how people operate when motivated by fear. They are obedient, diligent, and tied to the immediate task in front of them. They're doing all they can to avoid whatever painful result is hovering over their heads. But when the environment is hopeful rather than fearful, we find people operating with initiative, creativity, and passion. In that environment, they can perform at their best and companies have the best chance of maximizing their potential.

Fear comes from uncertainty and perceived danger. So, when the fundamentals of a company are sound, fear has a hard time taking root. That's why you find most healthy cultures attached to growing companies with a good business plan. For this reason, one of the best things you can do to create healthy environments for influence is first ensure the foundation and future of the company are solid. This will give your people confidence to fully engage with their talents.

However, since many of our readers will not be in the position to make those kinds of core company decisions, we want to point out another way to strengthen your foundation. Another force we find creating strong foundations even in companies experiencing difficulties are leaders who provide protection, direction and clarity for their people. These leaders are appropriately transparent giving clarity about the state of the company so people aren't left guessing. They provide direction so their teams know where they are going and what's expected of them. And they provide protection, doing all they can to protect their people from distraction, interruption and negative influences that can impede their progress. These leaders create a foundation of trust and hope even in the toughest environments where influence can begin to grow.

Step 2. Build the infrastructure where you, yourself, would like to work

Just as in creating an office building requires you to put good infrastructure and a solid roof on top of your foundation, so, too, a good culture needs solid infrastructure and roofing to create a safe environment were people can be at their best. Here are some tips for creating a solid infrastructure for your environment:

A. Hire the right people.

When you work with people that have the interests, skills, and drive you need for your organization, there's a greater chance for success. Jeff Bezos, CEO of Amazon, once offered warehouse employees up to $5,000 to quit their job. He wanted to make sure all of his employees actually wanted to be there. Fewer than 10 percent of those offered the buyout took it. If you hire the right people (and not just the nice people with the best résumés), you eliminate all kinds of issues, and have employees more likely to engage at a higher level.

B. Make sure they know what you expect.

Once you hire the right people, make sure the expectations are clearly stated. Your people aren't mind readers. Everyone wants to know how their work will be measured, so figure out a good way of communicating that to them.

C. Give them tools to do their work.

Give the people in your organization the tools they need to accomplish their work...and I'm not just talking about their computers. I'm talking about training, marketing, leadership, and creating the right corporate culture and positive and healthy work environment – all these tools will support the individuals in your organization, bring about hope, and create an environment of teamwork.

D. Tell them how they're doing.

People do their best when they know where they stand, and this kind of performance communication helps eliminate unnecessary fear. When people don't know where they stand, the uncertainty breeds defensive behavior, guessing, and chaos, where teams break down into frightened individuals. When people know how they're doing, it introduces confidence, direction, and progress.

E. Celebrate them when they perform or behave in exceptional ways.

If you hire the right people, give them clear direction, and pay them well for what they do, one of the best things you can do for them at that point is to recognize them for their achievements. There are few things that motivate well-paid, quality employees more than recognition.

Step 3. Design internal features that bring uniqueness and life

Great offices aren't just built on solid foundations with a strong infrastructure; they also have great internal features.

One of my friends recently visited a LinkedIn office in a major U.S. city. She told me about their cool office space with clean lines, exciting colors and neatly and strategically placed tall, standing desks . She was struck by the fact that these rows of standing desks were home to nearly all associates, from typical sales people to senior level leaders. The few rooms that existed on the floor, she said, were reserved for conferences, meetings, and offices for a few personnel. She got the sense that the

organizational structure in that building was flat and people of all levels have opportunity to contribute.

More than that, she said, the environment invites both work and play. Ping-Pong tables and huge pillow chairs created activity pockets on the floor and invited associates to change things up and get the creative juices flowing. As she followed the hallway through the working area into the break room she said she was blown away by what she found there. Stocked with a myriad of cereal varieties, fridges loaded with energy drinks and soda, and counters lined with food catered in by local restaurants, she got the impression, "They make it easy for people to *live* here!" And that is, in fact, the point. Because LinkedIn realizes so much of life and community these days happens at work, the company makes the most of that. They intentionally create a physical environment that delights their people and inspires them to be productive.

Southwest Airlines is another company famous for creating a physical environment that promotes flourishing. In their headquarters, there are open break areas on every floor, designated by a counter that looks like a plane wing, where Southwest employees are invited and encouraged to gather together. Whether it's an impromptu meeting, a birthday party, or a company celebration, these locations are a hub for culture building in their company. These spaces not only allow people to engage, they allow them to feel human. They cultivate an environment where influence and growth can take place – both at a company level and a personal level.

I know what you're thinking. "OK, but we're not LinkedIn or Southwest Airlines! How do we create spaces like that with the office we have?" Well, for those of you who have the ability to reshape your physical space, I have some tips on how you can create a more engaging physical environment. And if your physical environment is fixed, I have some tips on how you can cultivate a healthy cultural environment within your physical space.

I get a little geeky about office architecture. Several years ago when we were building our Symbolist office I studied Christopher Alexander's design principles and used those as a guide for the design and layout of our office. You know, most people can't tell you why they love a space when they walk into it. They just say "it feels good." But the truth is there are core design principles behind the creation of spaces people love. And interestingly, those physical design principles can also be metaphors for healthy cultural environments as well. So here are seven design principles for physical and cultural environments that feel good:

A. Paths and Goals: Have you ever noticed that in a garden, like the ones you'll find at a grand estate, there are clear cut paths that lead to a clearly defined and desirable end like a fountain or a tree? Physical indoor spaces that feel good have clearly defined paths that lead to desirable end goals. Think clean, open, interesting hallways that lead to an engaging break room or an updated workout facility.

Similarly, cultures that feel good have clearly defined career paths for their people and destinations along those paths that are exciting and desirable. When you know your leadership is intentionally helping you get where you want to go, it creates the kind of environment that feels good and people want to work in. Have you clearly marked the growth paths for your people?

B. Light from Two Sides: You've probably not noticed but all the rooms you've been in that feel "warm" have natural light sources from more than one wall. Whether there are windows on two adjacent walls or a window on one wall and a glass door letting in natural light from another room, if you want to have a room or space that feels good and is engaging, you need to have light from two sides.

Similarly, we find that employees value feedback from many sources. Getting insight from not just your boss but your peers on your performance, the value you add and where you can grow helps people see the bigger picture and how they fit within it. Healthy environments give you light from multiple sides. Does your culture provide feedback from different perspectives?

C. Staircase as a Stage: Remember the movie "Rocky"? Remember the famous scene where Sylvester Stallone runs up the steps at the end of a hard training and throws his hands into the air in victory? That staircase was his stage. In fact it continues to be, as a statue commemorating Rocky still stands at the top of the steps at the Art Museum in Philadelphia.

Staircases in physical spaces are most interesting when they are open and serve as a visible stage where the outside world can watch people reaching their desired destinations.

Similarly, in healthy cultural environments when people climb to new heights on a project, in the organization, or in personal goals, those achievements should be celebrated in the culture. People want to be seen when they grow and be celebrated for their growth. How are you doing that?

D. Activity Pockets: Remember those activity pockets we talked about at LinkedIn and Southwest Airlines? Those are gathering places that give employees a much-needed break to feel human and refuel to get back to work with renewed focus. And those places are needed to create healthy physical environments.

Similarly, leaders should be intentional about creating activity pockets in their team culture. What are the natural breaks in your culture where you can get your people together to have fun, connect as human beings, and be re-inspired by the mission you are on together?

E. Something Roughly in the Middle: Have you ever noticed that in big rooms that feel right there is always something roughly in the middle? Whether it's a large bouquet of flowers on a center table in a hotel lobby or a cluster of couches, big rooms that feel good, typically have an anchoring point or something "roughly in the middle."

Similarly, big cultures that feel good typically have values, attitudes, beliefs, or practices that are shared by all and serve as anchoring points. These values are the unspoken "something in the middle" of the culture that bring about unique cultural identity. Some cultures have "We work hard and play hard" at the middle of their culture. Some are all about creativity, ingenuity and spontaneity. Some exude the value of "Our people come first" and you can feel it.

What is in the middle of your culture? What values, attitudes, beliefs, and practices do you all have in common that shape your unique cultural identity? How can you celebrate those anchor points and use them to enhance your cultural brand?

F. Intimacy Gradients: Have you ever noticed that you typically lower your voice in rooms with lower ceilings or rooms that are smaller in general? In architecture, places of intimacy are designated by smaller spaces, tucked away and closed in a bit, providing privacy. People value these spaces because one-on-one conversation is needed just as team spaces are.

Similarly, cultural environments that feel good afford opportunity not just for large group or team connection but also one-on-one connection and feedback. Whether it's a boss connecting with an associate on a work matter or connecting with them as a human being, people want to be seen as individuals as well as a part of a collective. How are you making room for intimacy gradients in your culture and helping your people connect one-on-one as well as in a larger setting?

G. Street Windows: Often you'll find in office buildings that feel right, there is at least one big window, typically at the front, that gives a view to the street – whether it's a view to the parking lot, or a highway, or a park next door, physical spaces that feel good connect you to the outside world.

Similarly, cultures that feel good take time to lift their head up out of the weeds of their work and connect to the outside world. Whether it's a company community service day, or a field trip to a local business or cultural experience that can inspire or teach your people something helpful for their work, cultures that learn from and connect to the outside world are more relevant, healthier and stronger.

Once you have these unique internal features in place, you can decorate them with your own cultural flare. Roll out your proverbial carpet and paint your walls the colors that make you happy. Because these are the components that will make an environment a lasting place people want to be.

Finally, once you've done all that, consider the next step:

Step 4. Hang Out Your Sign

When you've done all that needs to be done on the inside of a building, you are finally ready to hang your logo on the outside. But remember this: Your internal brand will reflect on your external brand. Companies often think they can keep those separate, but they can't. When the internal components of a company are not healthy, eventually people on the outside will notice something is off. Similarly, when a company is fundamentally healthy internally, you won't be able to keep that from the outside world. The good news will leak out.

Therefore, whatever company logo or name you hang outside of your office building, we hope when your people see it they think to themselves, "That's my Turangawaewae."

Judith Campbell is a Pakeha (a Maori expression that means "white New Zealander"). She's on the very short list of several organizations, including the United Nations, as an expert at facilitating meetings for people in the midst of difficult, highly emotional circumstances. Name any hotspot on the planet, and it's likely that Judith has been called into that area to create a safe environment for dealing with a terrible situation.

I heard Judith speak not too long ago where she explained how she created an environment where progress could be made even among people holding dramatically different perspectives. It occurred to me that her insight also holds true for organizations desiring highly engaging workplaces. One thing she said resonated strongly with me: "Remember your Turangawaewae!"

Turangawaewae is the Maori term for "the place where I stand tall." A Turangawaewae in our situation is the kind of organization or department or boss who encourages their people to "stand tall." An environment with the practices and tools in place that support a culture and communicate to people that they matter. A Turangawaewae is a place where people are expected to engage to a greater degree because they are respected for their contributions.

If your company helps their people "stand tall," you will be surprised how their influence will grow stronger and more positive as time passes.

Ask yourself, "Does our culture and environment build people up and help them stand tall?" If not, what could you do to change that?

At the heart of these points is really one foundational truth:

Individuals matter.

Big organizations often lose sight of individuals because of the context of the big work they're trying to accomplish.

I've spoken with enough executives to realize they are, generally, really good, talented, intelligent people with good reasons why they've gotten to where they are. But they fall into the trap of running a business and believing everyone thinks like they do. They assume everyone is as passionate and interested in the business as they are. They assume people are content doing their work and will go on doing their work until the end of time.

They forget to take care of the individual.

They forget to implement systems that protect their people and the processes that offer them a voice.

Do you have all the foundational elements in place for a hopeful environment? Do you have the kind of cultural infrastructure you want to work in? Have you created a physical and cultural environment that "just feels good"? Do your people consider your brand a place where they can stand tall and be at their best for your company and themselves? Healthy community requires healthy environments.

LIFT

LIFT

6
Look in the Mirror

LIFT

During one of our sessions in Afghanistan, I asked the group of students one of my favorite questions:

"Who do you want to be when you grow up?"

They named the usual suspects: Lincoln, Gandhi, Mandela, as well as a few Afghan leaders.

"What do you know about Lincoln?" I asked. "Don't tell me about his accomplishments. Tell me about his life before he became president."

I got a lot of blank stares.

"Okay," I said. "Let me tell you about Abraham Lincoln, before he became President Lincoln. He grew up very poor. He was frequently defeated in politics, he had a child who died at a young age, and had a contentious relationship with his wife who struggled with mental illness as she aged. Then he was assassinated at age 56."

They looked at me, not sure what to say.

"Let's talk about Gandhi," I said. "He spent many years in prison and lived much of his life as an ascetic, taking long fasts both to purify his body and to protest injustice. He was assassinated at age 78 by three point-blank shots to his chest."

The facts started to sink in, but I continued.

"And how about Mandela? He spent 27 years in prison. Twenty-seven years! Much of that time was spent in a cement cell that measured eight feet by seven feet where he slept on a straw mat. When he was allowed outside, he and his fellow inmates spent their days breaking rocks into gravel. The glare from the lime permanently damaged his eyes."

By then I had their attention. They wanted to know where this was headed.

"Lincoln wasn't trying to be President Lincoln. He just did the work that was in front of him. The same can be said about Gandhi or Mandela. They didn't set out to be "great people" – they simply did the work that made sense in front of them. All three of them faced enormous difficulty but all three had perspectives on life they remained true to, and that's where they found their greatest area of influence."

My hope was these young, influential Afghans would realize the goal is not to imitate another person or to mimic exactly how another leader leads. The goal is knowing what they can do, recognizing their own talents, and then going and doing that. Their role might not be to pull Kabul up to first-world status – their role might be simply to go be a good father to their children, or a good mother, a great neighbor, an honest employer. Maybe as they do some self-exploration, they'll realize they have a talent for drawing or painting or photography. Once we find the area of our greatest talent, it will lead us into our greatest sphere of influence.

Too often we want to tell the next generation they can be anything they want to be, and it's just not true. Did you catch that? I know it's not a popular sentiment, especially among parents, but there are too many parents out there telling their children that if they practice basketball enough they'll be the next LeBron James. They tell their kids that if they get the right soccer coach, they can be the next David Beckham.

That's not just a lie; it's a horrid waste of time, effort and energy. We're all uniquely engineered to do something.

We all have talents specific to us, and no matter how hard we work at it, there are somethings we simply will not be able to do.

LeBron does what he does because he fits in the niche of what makes a successful basketball player, and then he goes out and works really, really hard at it. But the librarian who works at our library, who I love, who loves her job and who is good at what she does, what a waste of time if she tries to be the next LeBron.

There are roles of influence we all have, and they can best be understood in the context of how we've been made. Our strengths and weaknesses. Our interests. Our circumstances. Our talents.

> **"We all have talents specific to us, and no matter how hard we work at it, there are some things we simply will not be able to do."**

If you're breathing, you're here to do something. Sometimes the hard work is discovering what that something looks like, and then going out and doing it without measuring yourself against anyone else.

Some of you are reading this thinking, "I DON'T KNOW what I'm here to do! I don't know who I am or what I'm really good at! If you're in that spot, here are some tips you can use to get a better picture of who's looking back at you in the mirror and what type of work may be right in front of you.

1.) What have you always enjoyed doing, even as a child?

I always have enjoyed doing unique things, entrepreneurial things, even at a young age. At age nine I walked down to the corner drug store and asked the owner if I could get a job there. I wanted to save up for a drum set, and needed a way to make money.

Although he said *no*, looking back I realize, even then, I was making a connection between a need for money and how I could make it. I was showing entrepreneurial skills at age nine.

Years later my natural talents became apparent again while in college when I decided I would open my own used car dealership to pay for school. The idea appealed to me because, at the time in Texas, all that was necessary to get a dealership license (which allowed access to car auctions) was a lot, a sign and a phone. I took a picture of the Pizza Hut parking lot next to my house on the Baylor campus, painted "A1 Used Autos" on a sign and took a picture of that propped in a window of my house. My home phone served its purpose and, after sending in my application and $25, three weeks later I was officially in business.

Well, almost. I still needed a loan to get started. But I was only 20 years old – who would take me seriously? I sensed I needed to look legitimate, so I dressed in my only suit, bought a Parker pen for $3.25, stuck it in my pocket and confidently headed to all the banks in Waco. I talked to a half dozen bankers, explained my business plan and how much money I needed. They all smiled and said some version of, "No, I'm sorry. That won't work for us."

I expanded my search and went to a bank in Riesel – a small town 20 miles outside Waco. A man named Gary Welch was the bank president and he knew my family, though at that point I wasn't sure how well. I reviewed my plan with him, then sat there and waited for his response.

"Tom," he said, "I'm going to loan you the money, but not because of your business plan. I know your dad and your family, and I think you'll do fine with it. Remember this someday, when you're in the position to do it for someone else."

The $5,000 I borrowed turned into A1 Auto. I bought used cars that were in rough shape, got my mechanic friend to fix them up, then sold them for a profit. It helped me get through school, and I even sold a yellow, 1973 Ford pickup truck and used the profits to buy the engagement ring I used to propose to Catherine.

When you look back on your life, what are the skills and talents that consistently rise to the top in your story? Think of a few key moments when you felt most alive, when you did something really well and people around you affirmed it. What were you doing? What skill were you using? What was motivating you? What end goal was driving you? This line of thinking can help you uncover some of your core competencies and skills that will follow you throughout your lifetime.

Look in your own mirror.

- What childhood stories can you remember about yourself, and in which direction do they point you?

- Are you being true to the early signs of who you were going to be, or have you gone off in a totally different direction?

2.) What opportunities are in front of you?

Another line of thinking that can guide you is considering what opportunities are currently in front of you or are regularly offered to you. This can point to the kind of work you are skilled in, subject matter you enjoy and are considered proficient in, or the kind of work where you currently have mastery. These opportunities can show you where people see you adding value and therefore will easily look to you to contribute.

Maybe you're regularly asked to speak on a particular topic. Maybe when you write blog posts about certain issues you get a lot more hits than on others. Pay attention to the opportunities that keep repeating themselves. Pay attention to the times in life when you feel like you're running up against a brick wall.

Also, being mindful of the areas you are gravitating towards can be a good indication of the kind of skills or subject matter you want to use in the future. Maybe you're starting to notice all of your close friends are entrepreneurs, or artists, or into physical fitness. Maybe you are finding yourself picking up books on a particular subject. If these are aspirational areas of focus, areas where you don't yet have proficiency, consider whether you're willing to commit the effort necessary to develop in this kind of work. And if so, have you started the disciplines necessary to do so? Look carefully at yourself in the mirror.

Take a look at your circumstances.

- What skills do you find yourself continually using?

- What do you talk about, think about, dream about?

- What opportunities regularly present themselves to you?

- What kind of people do you continually surround yourself with?

- What aspirations do you have?

Take some time and think through those questions. Sit a while with your answers. They will tell you about where you are talented and how are you skilled. The easiest areas for you to grow in are the areas where you already have natural ability and talent. How can you lean into those strengths to increase your influence and impact where you are?

One thing you'll notice about mirrors – you can't choose the reflection. They will always reflect what's in front of them

Similarly, you can't choose what your talents will be; you can't choose where your influence will lie. If I decided to be an NBA player, I could spend the rest of my life shooting free throws and three-pointers and practicing passes, but I would never become an NBA player. It's just not in my mirror.

Some people might say, "I want to go work for Apple because they're innovative." But be honest with yourself – does Apple match your personality and skills? Because if you're not the right person for Apple, you won't have any fun there no matter how cool and innovative they are. Too many people try to shoehorn their way into a situation that looks attractive to them. If they were honest with themselves, they'd know very well they're not the right person for the task.

> **"One thing you'll notice about mirrors – you can't choose the reflection. They will always reflect what's in front of them."**

Look in your mirror. Who are you?

The last thing I would say about this is, you may have a natural talent or ability that will not necessarily be your profession. That's OK. The world is full of talented people who don't use all their talents in their jobs. Ideally you would like there to be a high correlation between your talents, passions, and job choices, but that's not always the case. When it's not, find opportunities to use those talents outside your work. If it keeps coming up in your mirror, then it's part of who you are, and you probably get a high level of satisfaction from using that skill. So, find ways to use it regardless.

3.) What do people who know you best say?

This next step is one few people do. Go to people who truly know you, who care about you, and ask them their perspective on you. What do they see as your skill set? What opportunities do they see regularly presenting themselves to you? What kinds of people do they see you spending quality time with? What do they see as your aspirations? What limitations would they say you have? What do they think you need to go to the next step?

Don't just ask your peers, ask people who are older than you, mentors, leaders, as well as people whom you lead. Ask them to give you honest feedback. This 360 degree evaluation exercise is not meant to tear you down, it's meant to help you understand your strengths and weaknesses and how you contribute.

Part of how we understand who we are and where we most add value is by asking the community of people around us.

Several years ago a friend of mine was making a decision to leave an organization that, as part of her role, afforded her the opportunity to speak to large audiences on a regular basis. In the process of making that decision, she sat down with a friend, who is an incredibly talented speaker himself and also a bit of a mentor, to ask his thoughts on her decision. Knowing her talent in this area and love for speaking, he challenged her choice. He reminded her that she was uniquely talented in this way and had been given an opportunity at this organization to use her talents. He was right; she recalled that much of the outside opportunities that continued to pop up for her revolved around speaking. For this reason, he encouraged her to negotiate a way where she could continue speaking for this organization on a part-time basis even after I left. I took his advice and am glad I did. That choice gave her the opportunity to continue refining her skills and enjoying the rewards of using her talents well.

Each time you consider a change to the career path you're on, ask people who know you best what they think about what you're considering. They will help you stay true to yourself.

4.) What do tests confirm about you?

Another great tool at our disposal for knowing our skills, personality, and what we bring to the table to influence others are assessment tests. For example, Gallup's **StrengthsFinders** assessment gives you a good idea where your primary skills lie. **The**

Birkman Method is a test used frequently by businesses to help employees maximize their performance. **Strong Interest Inventory** is a widely used assessment considered reliable in determining which career or occupational choices would be best for you based on your interests. And the **Myers-Briggs Type Indicator** helps identify your personality type.

These tests are helpful in giving you a broad understanding about who you are, your areas of strength, and, more importantly, your potential influence. But you will have to do the hard work of finding out how to apply these insights about who you are for maximum impact.

5.) What's most important to you?

The truth is, much of who we are is still in the making. And much of who we become and the choices we make is shaped by the vision we have for our lives. Most people let life happen to them. They never take time to truly take account of their hidden expectations for their lives and admit their dreams. But if you take time to identify those dreams, they can become important indicators of how you want to use who you are to influence, and what goals you want to accomplish with your life.

One of my favorite questions to ask people who are searching for their next move in life is to ask about their end destination. Sit across the conference room table or dinner table from me over a glass of wine and I may at some point ask you: "Tell me about your funeral." That may seem morbid to some, but it's a great exercise for determining your coordinates.

When someone asks you about your funeral, you may uncover some of your secret and even humorous expectations. You might have a particular song you'd like played or drinks and food you'd like served. Many people want no crying, only dancing. But most people, when they think about their funeral, think about who will be there and what they will say.

When you picture that day, look beyond the flowers and ask yourself, who do I want sitting in the chairs? Who do you want your life to have mattered to? If they were given a chance to stand and say a few words about you, what would you want them to say?

This can help you determine what you really want to accomplish with your life. Picture who is up on the podium telling the story of your life and how it forever shaped theirs. What contributions of your life do you want them to talk about? How do you want them to sum up your life and your impact? This will help you think through the big objectives of your life and whether you are heading in the right direction.

Who do you want carrying your casket? Who are the people you want walking beside you in life and in death? As we've discussed, you create community in many different areas of life: in your home, in your neighborhood, at your work, and at the places you play. But who are the most important people, and are you prioritizing them?

Finally, when you get to the gravesite where you'll be laid to rest, if you could pick one sentence that summed up your life and what you meant to the world, what would you want it to say?

When you ask questions like this, hopefully you'll begin to see that you do have expectations for not just what you want to do with your life but how you want your life to matter to others. You already have expectations for your influence. So what are they? How do you want your life and skills to influence others? Take a moment to answer the questions

below for the first time, or maybe the hundredth, chart a clear direction for where you want to go.

- Who do you want to be at your funeral? Who do you want

your life to have mattered to?

- If they were given a chance to stand and say a few words about you, what would you want them to say?

- Who is up on the podium telling the story of your life? How do you want them to sum up your life and your impact?

- Who do you want carrying your casket? Who are the people you want walking beside you in life and in death and are you prioritizing them?

- What does your tombstone say? What is the one sentence summing up your life and impact?

We all want to be able to answer the question, "Do I matter?" with, "Yes, I do matter." We come to that conclusion through honest self-evaluation confirmed by third-party input. It takes a village to confirm how we are made, what we're good at, and help us become the people we have the potential to be. So what does it look like for you to take the next step in developing your character?

LIFT

7

Strengthening Your Personal Brand

LIFT

Once you have a broad understanding of who you are and the impact you want your life to have, how do you go about achieving that?

First, you must distill your vision into practical components. One great way to do this is by enlisting the help of someone like a career coach. Often coaches will help you determine your "Personal Mission Statement" to think more tactically about the specific goals you want to pursue in achieving your life mission.

Often the first session is a complete diagnostic, 90 minutes of groundwork, preparing the foundation for you to move forward. One friend recently told me about her life changing experience of hiring a career coach. She said she arrived at their initial meeting prepared with a list of jobs and companies she would be interested in and a list of her skills. She walked into the session and laid all of this information on the table in front of her coach.

Her coach smiled. Pushing all the information to the side she said, "This is all really neat. But let's start with something else." Her coach put a piece of paper with a simple stick figure of a woman in front of her and said, "Let's pretend this is you at 60. Who is this woman?" Don't just think career. Think about her whole life. What does she look like physically? How is she emotionally? What adjectives describe her? What is in her life and what's not: friends, family, children? What characterizes her life, does she travel, have a house, have a dog? What has she accomplished up to this point in career and in impact and what is she doing now in the second half of her life?"

During the following weeks, my friend and her coach worked through those questions. Some were easy to answer. Others, not so much. But all of them helped her identify the practical goals she had for her life. Then she started charting them on a timeline. She determined what she wanted to accomplish in the next five weeks, five months, and five years, personally and professionally.

Those answers now serve both as targets for my friend to go after and guardrails that keep her heading in the right direction.

Let's start breaking your life vision into practical goals:

- What are your health goals: What do you want your physical and emotional health to look like?

- What are your relational goals: What do you want for your marriage, family, friends, community?

- What are your financial goals: What are your goals for savings, a house, car, vacations, etc.?

- What are your career goals: Where do you want to go in your career? What do you want to achieve?

- What are your purpose goals: How do you want to have made an impact in others lives?

Now ask yourself: **When** do you want to accomplish these objectives? **What** do you want to do in the next five weeks, five months, five years. **Who** can you ask who can keep track of those aspirations with you and serve as an accountability resource to help you achieve your dreams? Often we don't get to where we want to go because we don't have someone holding our feet to the fire of our dreams. If you want something, you have to go after it, and you have to have help!

What do you do when you don't know how to get there?

Many of us, when we recognize what our goals are, we realize that in order to achieve them we're going to need some help.

No matter who we are or where we are in life, we are all heading somewhere. Usually, it's somewhere we've never been before. Maybe you're looking to rise to a certain level in your company, or maybe you're trying to get to a place of proficiency in your career. Maybe you're trying to achieve a financial milestone you haven't yet reached and the truth is, you simply don't know how.

You're looking for a map and you can't find it. But what you may not realize is, no matter where you are, there are people all around you. Some of them have been to the places you want to go. And they know how to help you get there – so ask them for help!

When I don't know how to do something I often ask two questions:

1. Who do I know who can help me?

2. How else can I learn what I need to know?

General Network:

Whether it's how to train for triathlons, how to cook, or the best places to visit in a city, learning from the people you know makes your life infinitely easier and better! Take a look at your goals. Who do you know who has gotten to the places you want to go? If you don't know anyone who has gotten to your particular goal, who in your network is most likely to know someone who has reached your goal? Ask them.

Mentors:

One of the primary ways I see people developing in life is through mentors. To find a mentor I look within my current network. Who are the women or men who are in the places of life I aspire to be? Who has the kind of character, competencies, and relational life I admire? If I don't know anyone like that, I ask my network who they know. When I determine who I think would be great to learn from, I'll ask to buy them coffee or lunch and pick their brain about how they got where they are. Sometimes that simply goes down as a one-time informational interview. And sometimes that buds into a friendship where I can ask that person to meet with me from time to time and give me tips as I'm pursuing similar goals.

- Here are a couple things to note about mentors:

- Have more than one. You can wear people out if they're your solo go-to person.

- Be respectful of their time. Keep it to a set block of time and come with questions prepared.

- Find a way to say *thank you* creatively. Maybe a note. Maybe a spontaneous gift, book or chocolates. Help them see that you value them!

- Ask them how you can help them. Remember the balcony exercise?

Sponsors:

One critical way I see people developing in their careers is by having internal sponsors within their company. Researchers say sponsorship is the most important factor in determining who advances to the highest corporate levels. The vast majority of C-level leaders have all had at least one internal mentor or coach; someone who not only helped them find opportunities to grow but also coached them through different circumstances and advocated for them to leadership.

You can gain internal sponsors by being intentional about finding ways to connect with leaders and demonstrating your passion about adding value to the organization.

Here are some tips in finding sponsors:

- Take advantage of opportunities to build relationships outside your department through company golf teams, service activities, etc. and develop relationships with leaders who could advise or support you down the road.

- Volunteer for a company project alongside more senior leaders. Do good work, and when you've established relationship and credibility with them, ask for their help and advice on how you can grow your career and add even more value.

- Make other people look good. If someone advocates for you internally, do especially good work. Your good reputation will reflect positively on them and cause others to want to advocate for you too.

Outside learning:

Ask yourself what additional learning opportunities you have access to. These could be through industry associations, certifications, conferences and training seminars. Often, larger companies have formal learning opportunities in either a leadership network or classes they host on campus. What projects can you participate in that can give you needed experience in an area where you're lacking – whether inside your organization or in your community?

Let's review. Confirm with yourself and someone you trust:

- Here's what I think I'm built to do and able to do.

- Here's what I want to accomplish with my life.

- This is a list of people I know who can help.

- Here are the resources I have to help me get there.

- This is what I'm already doing to get there.

- Here are the opportunities I have in front of me to go farther.

- And, finally, here's what I need to go do.

It's not just about what you do, it's also about the way you do it.

I was in Chicago and I was looking for a cab. Any cab would have been fine. Fortunately for me, I didn't end up in just any cab – I ended up in the cab driven by "The Best Cab Driver in Chicago." His name was Moon S. Choi, and he gave me a quick glimpse into just how influential you can be by doing a few, small things right.

The car itself was fine, not spectacular, and the outside of it wouldn't have jumped out at you if you were walking down the street. But as I crawled into the car, I blurted out my destination and Mr. Choi repeated it back to me, tagging on a "Yes, thank you." That got my attention. The car pulled into the traffic, and that's when I started to take in my surroundings. The inside of his cab was like no other cab I had ever ridden in.

First he had classical music playing at just the right volume, not too quiet, not too loud. The inside of the car was immaculate, and I noticed the handle of a small, hand-held vacuum under the front seat. There was a fresh bottle of water in the side of both back doors, along with a pad of receipts. Then I noticed the piece of paper taped to the side of the back door.

"VOTED CHICAGO'S BEST CAB AND BEST
CAB DRIVER IN 2010!"

He was clearly proud of his accomplishment.

By that time during my stay in Chicago, I had traveled to and from the McCormick Center dozens of times and I was very familiar with the normal cab route. I knew what the fare would be, within a dollar or so (based on the traffic). Mr. Choi, however, took a different route than normal that turned out not only to be quicker but also 25 percent less expensive – it was even a more scenic route, (although I'm assuming he took it simply because it was the fastest). Maybe he was just so good that he could throw the scenery in for the fun of it.

When I arrived at my destination, I paid Mr. Choi, tipping him much more than I normally did. I told him I was honored to be driven by "The Best Cab Driver in Chicago," and I asked if I could take his picture. Then I made sure I had his cab number and the phone number for the place to call with comments. One more vote for Mr. Choi!

I was reminded, through Mr. Choi, that being influential isn't just about what you do; it's about *the way* you do it. Mr. Choi knew his skills and opportunities and cultivated a vision for the kind of cab experience he wanted for his customers. Then he brought his vision to life with intentionality and excellence and it caused him to stand out among his peers.

The experiences we create for people when they encounter our work and us as people begins to build a reputation about us in the community. This reputation, or as we call it personal brand, can either restrict our capacity to influence or expand it.

Building your personal brand

Our company recently led an **Influence Workshop** for a group of professionals at a Fortune 500 company. We discussed principals like:

- The best way to gain influence with others is to help meet *their* needs first.

- Gaining help from influential people requires that we be the kind of people they *want* to help.

That last one requires that you have a strong personal brand. I break brand into three parts: Trust, Love, and Presentation.

1. Trust

You must be a person of competency and consistency. You can't just know your stuff; you must do good work. People need to know they can rely on you to take care of them and represent their brand well – whether that's the company's brand or a leader's personal brand they put on the line to recommend you. If someone spends their financial or relational capital on you, they want to know it will pay dividends. Here's a quick litmus test to see how you're doing on trust:

- Do you show up on time?

- Do you follow through on your commitments?

- Do you deliver a good product?

- Do you say what you mean and mean what you say? Do you under-promise and over-deliver?

- Do you admit when you make a mistake and take immediate measures to correct it?

2. Love

Love is the 4-letter word we don't say at work. But the truth is you need it to be successful at work. To be truly successful, you cannot just be a person who has skills and expertise, you also must be a person who works well with others and treats people, regardless of their role, with dignity, respect, and care.

Kevin Roberts, former CEO and current Executive Chairman of the branding firm, Saatchi and Saatchi, says truly successful *brands,* brands that are not just liked by customers but beloved, have two variables in common: respect and love. They are respected for their consistent product quality, but they are loved because they "see" their customers. They connect with them as human beings and inspire them. Influential people do the same.

Think of the best leaders of your life, you know, the coach, teacher, boss you'd "take a bullet for." Were they influential to you because of their IQ or skill? That may have been *part* of it. But wasn't it the way they believed in you, challenged you, encouraged you, affirmed you, and inspired you to be all you could be that made them beloved in your life? Me, too. We call this emotional intelligence. And experts are saying EI is as critical to leadership these days as IQ and Skill. How are you doing at loving those in your community? Here are some questions to consider:

- Do you genuinely care about the people you engage with?

- Do you connect with them at a human level?

- Do you know what they care about, what they are good at, and what they're striving to achieve. And do you find ways to encourage, affirm and even help them?

- Do you find ways to inspire them to do even greater things?

3. Presentation

The way you stand, dress, and speak in front of others matters. You can be the most trustworthy and emotionally intelligent person on earth but if you don't represent well publicly, they won't be inclined to push you out in front. Remember when someone influential recommends you, you're reflecting their brand.

- Do you dress the part and act the part you're being asked to play?

- Do you speak confidently and articulately in front of others?

- Do you carry yourself well? How is your body posture and your handshake? How are your conversation skills?

The truth is, most people I know, no matter how savvy, desire help with these things. And the good news is, you can improve your presentation skills in all of these areas.

My friend who does presentations to large audiences asks a fashion conscious friend to coach her on what she wears. In time, with instruction, my friend has developed enough skill at wardrobe choices to feel confidant in making selections on her own. However, she still double checks with these friends before big events just to be sure.

Another friend coaches professionals regularly on presentation skills, whether for meetings, speeches or general engagement. He asserts that many professionals are incredibly bright and competent but don't know how to present well and it diminishes their credibility. It's amazing what a coach and some good basic instruction can do to improve your presentation game.

As you gain ground in these areas, it won't just impact your brand, you will strengthen your confidence. And that can change your opportunities.

How is your personal brand? Where do you see opportunity to strengthen it? Are there areas where you need to grow in knowledge, skill, or competency? How can you do that? Are there people with whom you need to cultivate relationships for further growth? Do you need to work on your level of trust or love within your community? Do you need to work on your personal presentation skills? What is your plan to strengthen your personal brand?

LIFT

LIFT

8
The Power of Choice

LIFT

You don't have to go back too far to find a time when people didn't have choice. In fact, there are many parts of the world today where choices are limited and based more on survival than anything else. There are millions of people whose only worry right now is scavenging for their next meal – maybe their only meal of the day. They don't have the luxury of sitting down and spending time wondering about how to increase their influence. They aren't concerned with building a following on Facebook or Twitter. They wake up hungry, and in their minds they go down the list of possible food sources. Their choices, in every aspect of life, are severely limited, and oftentimes even nonexistent.

An extreme case of non-choice would be human trafficking, people who are stuck in a situation in which they have no choice whatsoever. They go where they are told, they eat what they are given, and they do exactly as they are instructed. Even their bodies are not their own – some are sold for sex, others for manual labor. Then they sleep for a few short hours before waking up and starting all over again.

Choice is part of the new paradigm of influence, so if you live in the western world and you are reading this book, then you probably have a choice. You probably make hundreds of choices every day, choices that usually have nothing to do with life or death and won't impact whether you have food on the table at the end of the day. You decide what time to wake up, what kind of coffee to drink, what to have for breakfast. You decide which roads to take to work and how hard to work that day. You get home and decide what to watch on the television or what books to read or music to listen to.

Our lives are oceans filled with choices.

But only a handful of choices are important ones, choices that will determine your direction in life, choices that have the potential to make a huge impact on those around you. Some of those important choices are these:

- Choosing what to create with your life and talent.

- Choosing when and where to add value.

- Choosing who you will influence and how.

- Choosing which community in which to invest.

To help you make these choices strategically, consider the following tips to "unstick" your decision-making process and frame your big decisions well.

1. Multi-Track a Few Options

Whether you are trying to decide whether or not to go to graduate school for further development or choosing whether to go with one solution or another on a project, making big choices can seem overwhelming. People often feel paralyzed by choices when there simply are too many of them.

Have you ever noticed that the sales associate in Nordstrom's shoe department typically only brings out two or three choices for you to consider rather than the 12 they have in that size and color? That's because research tells us that when we offer people too many choices, their ability to choose and their satisfaction with the choices they make diminishes. This is why retailers and marketers will often display a limited set of choices to buyers so they will increase both frequency and satisfaction of purchases.

If you find yourself paralyzed by an ocean of choices, select two or three good options that will get you closer to your goal and begin pursuing those. This may mean walking through the strengths and weaknesses of various solutions and trying them out before you buy in, or considering the value of on the job experience verses more schooling. This may mean keeping your full-time job and pursuing a small business interest in your free time to see if your concept gains momentum.

Often choices that lead to big change require time and data gathering so it can be beneficial to multi-track, or simultaneously pursue a few options, and see which fits best.

2. Do the Next Thing

From the outside, often we look at big decisions someone makes in life and conclude that it takes a lot of courage to make those kinds of decisions. Does it take a lot of courage to take out a second mortgage on your home and start a new business? Does it take a lot of courage to step away from a secure day job and enter the scary realm of self-employment? Does it take a lot of courage to walk across the street and talk to a stranger, or to make a call to set up a meeting with someone you've been wanting to meet with for a long time?

Those things all may look courageous from the outside, but I would argue that, to the person making the choice, making the change, it's not so much courageous as it is the next logical step. They are following their circumstances and taking the next step in embracing their opportunities.

Some people may have looked at me starting a new company and thought, "Wow, that takes a lot of guts. Why doesn't he just find a good job that pays well and has retirement benefits?" Some people think that was an extremely courageous thing.

But it didn't seem like a courageous thing to me – it just felt like the right next thing to do based on the combination of all the circumstances in my life at the time. It seemed like the next logical step.

So in regard to the changes you want to make, what is the next logical step?

- If you want to write a book but can't seem to find the time, the next logical step for you could be to wake up an hour earlier and set a word count goal for each morning.

- If you're working on a project and keep running into the same roadblock, "the next thing" for you could be to determine three potential solutions and start exploring them.

- If you want to grow in experience and competency for your career, "the next step" for you could be to sign up for an extra project in your company that can grow your experience and skill.

- If you continue to see a need in the marketplace and you've thought you could create a solution for that need, a next step could be to do a competitive analysis and start writing a business plan.

Based on where you want to go, what is the next logical thing you can do to get closer to achieving your goal?

3. See Failure As Part of the Pathway to Success

One of the biggest barriers to choice is fear. We fear difficult conversations. We fear hearing the word "no." We fear going out on a limb and proposing our ideas to others. We fear these things because we ultimately fear failure and rejection. And those fears can leave us inactive. But we must ask ourselves: If we do nothing, will be satisfied with staying in our current situation or is the pain great enough that we are willing to start following our opportunities, reaching out, and doing the work needed to get where we want to go?

Sara Blakeley graduated from FSU with a degree in communications. After college, she took a job working for Danka selling fax machines door-to-door. She flourished in sales at Danka and was promoted early to national sales trainer at age 25.

"If we do nothing, will be satisfied with staying in our current situation or is the pain great enough that we are willing to start following our opportunities, reaching out, and doing the work needed to get where we want to go?"

In her role, Sara had to wear pantyhose in the hot Floridian climate. She didn't like the appearance of a seamed foot with open toed shoes but she did like the way the control-top made her body look. Once for a private party, she experimented by cutting off the feet of her pantyhose and wearing them under a new pair of slacks and found they still achieved the desired result.

All of a sudden Sara had an idea. She realized there was a need in the marketplace and she could meet it. Don't you think Sara faced fear at this point? What if she tried hard and failed? What if she proposed her idea and was rejected?

Sara spent the next two years and $5,000 of her savings researching and developing her hosiery idea. When she had trouble finding a patent lawyer she learned how to write her own patent from a textbook she found at Barnes & Noble. She drove to the state of North Carolina where most of America's hosiery mills existed and proposed her idea to multiple decision makers. She was turned down by every company. But failure and rejection didn't stop her. Two weeks after she returned home, a male mill operator based in Asheboro, North Carolina called Sara and offered to try out her concept. After Sara's departure, the man's two daughters encountered Sara's prototype and strongly encouraged him that this idea was a winner.

How did Sara get over fear and rejection to accomplish her dream? She gives credit to a question her father used to ask her each day after school when she was a child. He asked, "So, what did you fail at today?" Sara's father saw failure not as an end or as a catastrophic outcome, but as a data point necessary for learning.

He encouraged his daughter to learn this concept so she would get comfortable with the fear of rejection and failure, go after her goals, and learn how to succeed.

Sara's choice to see failure as a part of the process, not only gave her the courage to bring a great product to market, it also gave her incredible success. Sara is the founder of Spanx. And because of her courage Sara has become one of the world's youngest self-made billionaires.

What if you saw failure as a learning opportunity rather than a catastrophe, a pathway to success rather than an end?

Could that help you overcome fear and choose to pursue the next logical step?

4. Mind Your Mind

So much of success is determined by what goes on between our ears. Business leaders know this. Sports psychologists know this. We all, deep down, know this. We naturally get into patterns of self-defeating thoughts and paralyze ourselves with thoughts of our inadequacy or past failures. As a result we opt out of choosing because it's easier not to. Because we fear the unknown, we talk ourselves out of making the bold decisions that can change lives.

But it doesn't have to be that way. There is a lot of neuroscience that has come out in the last decade around the idea of Neuroplasticity. Neuroplasticity is the discovery that the mind can change the brain. We can change our patterns of thinking and, as a result, our choices by intentionally focusing on and controlling what we think. Overcoming fear and patterns of self-defeating thoughts require a new kind of thinking.

We recently consulted with a small company that helps non-profits raise money. It turns out their clients deal with a lot of fear about asking donors for money. We talked about three simple steps that could help their clients develop a new kind of thinking and give them the courage to do the work in front of them:

Reframe

Similar to our last tip, in fearful circumstances we need to reframe the way we see rejection and disappointment. A good question to ask when you encounter failure is, "What does this make possible?" Reframe your view of circumstances to see disappointment not as an end in itself but the beginning of a new set of opportunities.

Think of the potential failures you face in making the choices in front of you. How can you reframe those challenges to the see opportunity that could come from failure rather than the obstacles?

Remember

An emotional intelligence coach I know who works with senior executives taught me that the antitoxin of the brain is *gratitude*. He reminds me that when we encounter difficulty, our brain secretes Cortisol, a chemical that sends us into fight or flight behavior – certainly not a great condition from which to make decisions. But gratitude flushes Cortisol out of the brain with positive chemicals like Serotonin and Dopamine. He teaches executives to think back to past successes with gratitude as a way of controlling their fear and anxiety and be more effective under stress.

As you encounter fear in choosing, what past successes can you remember with gratitude to flush out the stress chemicals present in your brain and gain courage and clarity for moving ahead?

Repeat

One of my friends in business development keeps a note on his desk that says simply, "Some will. Some won't. So what. Someone's waiting." He reminds himself daily of the truth that some people will need what he offers and some won't. By remembering this, he has already decided not to let disappointment hold him back from pursuing those who are waiting for what he has to offer.

What are the truths you need to repeat to yourself to overcome fear and go after what you want? Maybe you need to remind yourself of what you're good at. Maybe you need to speak your goals out loud on a regular basis. Maybe you need to commit to remind your colleagues or neighbors of those truths when you encounter difficulty.

5. Realize It Won't Go Exactly According To Plan

I believe the amount of influence you are able to have will be directly proportional to your ability to embrace all your life's circumstances – how and where you were brought up as a child; your physical and mental limitations; your schooling; your talents; your friends; the disasters and victories you experienced. All of these will shape who you are and who you influence.

If you embrace the circumstances of your life, you will have a huge influence on others. If you fight the circumstances and try to force your life in a direction it wasn't meant to go, then you will spend the majority of your time planning for things that will probably never happen, making lists of goals you will probably never achieve, and obsess with huge amounts of jealousy over people in the world who are living the life you wanted to live.

Embrace your circumstances, go where they lead you, and you will find your greatest sphere of influence. But how can we live this way, when this way of living practically guarantees that tomorrow will hold a new set of challenges? How do we make decisions when we've committed to following circumstances? Are we even making decisions, or are we simply allowing things to happen to us?

How do we respond to these challenges?

Here's my take. First of all, run toward the challenges. Don't avoid them. Don't delay making decisions. Sprint toward the tough stuff, and then you'll figure it out before anyone else does.

Challenges also are easier to deal with when you are a whole person. By this I mean, don't be a one-dimensional being, focused totally on work or education or that "Number One" goal. Make time to create relationships that are meaningful. Have a hobby you daydream about. Be excellent at work, yes, but also figure out what you need in order to live a passionate life and then aggressively pursue that life.

Hang around good people who do cool stuff. Contribute to their circumstances in a way that impacts them and in a way that leads them to say you're a good person who is also doing cool stuff. This contributes to that ripple effect, that never-ending impact that will increase your influence.

Finally, when you're confronted with challenges, forget about how you did it yesterday. Embrace your current circumstances when trying to solve current problems. Come up with the best way to do it *today*, and don't rely on past victories.

One of the coolest things that comes out of embracing circumstances, while keeping your end goals in mind, is you'll develop the ability to manage something called emergent work. I think a lot of what we encounter in life can be dealt with well when we deal with it in an emergent way. In other words, see what happens. Go with the flow. Follow the opportunities that present themselves. Plan as much as possible, but then go and see what happens.

The opposite of this would be going into a situation with such completely thought out, rigid plans that you refuse to adjust, even when an exciting opportunity presents itself.

It's important to approach life with this emergent work mentality. We have to be willing to see what opportunities will arise. It's the unknown nature of the results, the ripples spreading outward, that make life exciting and expand our influence. You'll know when to move forward when you're confronted with an opportunity and you know that if you don't do that particular thing, it would bother you and seem like a wasted chance.

I went to Afghanistan not because I had a huge love for the Middle East, not because I had always wanted to speak about influence in another country, and not because I was looking for an organization that would help me travel around the world. In fact, I had never considered traveling to Afghanistan. Never. But circumstances had it that I became friends with Ross, and we had some common passions, and, eventually, he asked me if I'd like to go to Afghanistan with him.

Often times the right way to go is the way that's right in front of you. Following the emergent work in your life gets easier as you get into the habit. I feel like I know how to do it now, and it comes with a huge sense of adventure.

So no, it's not going to go exactly the way we plan, but when we keep the vision for our lives in mind and hold the *how* with an open hand, we can be surprised by unexpected wonder.

6. Prepare Well for Risk Taking

Yes, courage and choice are necessary to getting where we want to go. And, yes, taking risks is a natural part of that process. But there are some preparatory steps you can take that make taking those risks easier and less fearful. Here are some of those steps to take:

A. Remember your foundational beliefs

Whether we've stated them explicitly or not, we all have core values; principles about us and who we want to be that are embedded in our DNA. In good times and in bad, these beliefs will guide you. And in making decisions they can drive you to live the life you want. Know your foundational core values and the mission statement of your life. Write them down. Stick to them. And let them propel you to become the person you want to be.

B. Healthy cash reserves buy time

Having access to cash makes all the difference in difficult times. Trouble is at hand when aggressive financial decisions in boom cycles don't prepare for downturns. Having cash when others don't creates opportunities and gives you time to adjust.

C. Relationships are critical

Often when people are in real trouble it's because they are relationally stranded on an island. They have not put in the relational investments necessary to make withdraws in times of need. Make sure you're consistently keeping relationships top priority.

D. Maintain personal health and perspective

When trouble comes we often forget the habits that give us life and help us keep things in perspective. For many, these habits include exercise, reflecting, eating right, and connecting with family and friends. Be disciplined to do the things that keep you healthy and give you life. You will need it in every season.

E. Your daily habits will shape your life

In her book *The Writing Life*, Pulitzer Prize winning author, Annie Dillard, reminds us: "How we spend our days is how we spend our lives...A schedule defends from chaos and whim. It is a net for catching days." What are your routines? What kind of days are you creating?

Embarking down the road of "choice," going after what you want, requires facing your fear, minding your thinking, preparing well, and holding the outcomes with an open hand. But it is also a road full of life-giving experiences you will never have if you just stay where you are. So embrace the power (and adventure) of choice.

LIFT

LIFT

9
Go Do

LIFT

As we sit here, there are people starting their run for political office, people starting charities that will revolutionize the lives of underprivileged people. People are opening businesses right now, as we speak. Someone out there is rescuing young girls from sex trafficking. Someone else is teaching a child to read, or opening a gym, or meeting with a venture capitalist.

There are stories of influence being written right now.

What story are you writing?

So often we get overwhelmed by big stories of influence and think we're not capable of creating stories that grand in our own lives. We forget that great influence comes from a lifetime of small choices. See, the truth is, your choices don't have to be huge to be influential. They simply need to be intentional and you have to have the courage to make them.

Here are some things we want to remind you of and encourage you with as you're out there making choices and influencing people:

1. Influence is NOT networking.

I know what you're probably thinking:

But Tom, you made a big deal about making connections and getting involved in the lives of those around you. Isn't that the same thing as networking?

Influence and networking may look a lot alike, but if you drill down a little you'll see some major differences. To be honest, I'm not a fan of the word, "networking" or the motivations behind it. Networking has kind of taken on a life of its own, and now there's even an entire business model that revolves around it: network marketing. The definition most people have of networking is that they need to go meet people because they themselves will benefit from these new connections, somehow using the new relationship to grow their business or their brand.

Don't get me wrong. That's fine. I fully understand the benefit of meeting new people and why one would want to increase the size of one's personal network. But the underlying foundation of networking is always self-centered – I'm making these connections for me, to grow *my* business, to increase *my* audience.

Influence is very different. If I'm trying to grow my area of influence, I would prefer to say that I'm going to meet with people to see what happens, to see where their connections and goals intersect with my own. Can I add value to what they are pursuing?

If you are using the networking model, you will email people and say, "We should meet," and your motivation for meeting will be to make a connection that benefits yourself. If you are genuinely concerned with influence, you'll email someone and say, "I think it makes sense for us to meet for these reasons, and I think it could potentially benefit both of us for these reasons. If this makes sense to you, let's meet."

Do you see the difference? Influence is more about connecting with people and trusting that they have the same needs that I have, either from a personal or a business standpoint. Networking is more about squeezing every ounce of benefit that we can from any given relationship or potential relationship.

The fact is, influence will always be more effective than networking, because people will always respond more to this kind of reaching out than a simple networking opportunity.

Be an influencer, not a networker.

2. Influence is NOT leadership.

Merriam Webster has three primary definitions for leadership:

- a position as a leader of a group, organization, etc.

- the time when a person holds the position of leader

- the power or ability to lead other people

The reason that it's important that we don't equate influence with leadership is that often leadership is limited to one position within a group of people. The President of the United States. The governor of a state. The principal of a school. The captain of a team.

Those are all examples of leadership positions, some elected, some chosen. Do you see the problem with equating leadership with influence? If influence equals leadership, then none of the other team members can have any influence; none of the teachers or students can influence each other; the citizens of a state or a nation cannot have influence. Only people in leadership positions can influence.

And we know that's not true.

Influence is not leadership. It's not limited to those in leadership positions. Besides, influence doesn't look the way most of us think leadership looks.

Many times, leadership has more ties with the old paradigm of influence than with the new. Leadership involves hierarchy and organizational charts and bosses.

Influence doesn't have to involve any of those things. Influence can be held by the person stocking shelves as well as the CEO, by the janitor as well as the principal. Influence takes place every day, in every community, regardless of Possessions or Pedigree or Position.

Influence is not leadership.

One of the most influential people I know of was never what

you would call a "leader." Day after day, for most of her 87 years, a woman in Mississippi collected dirty clothes and returned them clean. It was her job after all – she was a laundry lady. That's all she had ever done. She left school in the 6th grade and never got married. She never had any children. She never got her driver's license, and the farthest away she ever traveled was to Niagara Falls, which she found terrifying.

Her name was Osceola McCarty, and she was a saver. As the years passed, she continued washing people's clothes and lived a very simple life. Every extra nickel, quarter, dollar she made, she put in a savings account. She spent almost nothing. She lived in her old family home, rarely bought new shoes and even taped Corinthians into her Bible to keep it from falling out.

Over the years she saved $150,000.

In 1995, her banker asked her what she wanted them to do with all of her money when she died, and she told them she wanted to set up a scholarship fund at the University of Southern Mississippi in her town, where tuition was $2,400 a year. So she did.

"I wanted to share my wealth with the children," Miss McCarty said. "I never minded work, but I was always so busy, busy. Maybe I can make it so the children don't have to work like I did."

People in Hattiesburg call her donation "The Gift."

Talk about influence! For nearly 80 years Miss McCarty was doing other people's laundry, and do you think they considered her to be an influential person? Do you think they looked at her and thought, *She's going to change the world?* Probably not. She didn't have a fancy title. She didn't lead a company or a team. But was she influential? Undoubtably.

Do you know that concept of never-ending impact? Well, Miss McCarty's donation showed up on the radar of philanthropists and foundations across the country. News media flocked to her humble home, where they interviewed her (she turned on the air conditioning for them, something she had bought a few years before and used only when company was in the house). Her story spread.

Leaders in Hattiesburg joined together in the wake of Miss McCarty's unexpected donation and decided to match it, doubling her efforts. Bill Pace, the executive director of the University of Southern Mississippi Foundation, found it hard to believe.

"I've been in the business 24 years now, in private fundraising," Mr. Pace said. "And this is the first time I've experienced anything like this from an individual who simply was not affluent, did not have the resources and yet gave substantially. In fact, she gave almost everything she has. No one approached her from the university; she approached us. She's seen the poverty, the young people who have struggled, who need an education. She is the most unselfish individual I have ever met."**

The immediate ripple effect of her donation was that it doubled, becoming a $300,000 fund called, "The Osceola McCarty Scholarship Fund." Her influence motivated local business leaders to get involved. And the ripple didn't stop there.

As a young woman, Stephanie Bullocks' mother wanted to go to the University of Southern Mississippi. But that was during the height of the integration battles, and if she had tried, her father might have lost his job with the city.

It looked as if Stephanie's own dream of going to the university would also be snuffed out, for lack of money. Although she was president of her senior class in high school and had grades that were among the best there, she fell just short of getting an academic scholarship. Miss Bullock said her family earned too much money to qualify for most federal grants but not enough to send her to the university.

Then, last week, she learned that the university was giving her $1,000, in Miss McCarty's name. "It was a total miracle," she said, "and an honor."

Miss McCarty wasn't bothered that there are people who gave

more to universities than she did. She didn't seem to mind that her donation wouldn't pay for EVERY young person who wanted to attend the university. She wasn't stopped by her humble beginnings. She wasn't a leader. But, man, how she influenced.

3. Influence isn't "making the most of every opportunity." It's making the most of *your* opportunity.

The price of being fully alive is knowing where your primary areas of influence are and then walking away from secondary areas that take up too much time or distract you from your primary area of influence. Once you see where your influence lies, you will be confronted with a choice to enter into that situation or to continue engaging in areas where you don't have influence.

This can be difficult because for some people this might mean taking a lower-paying or less prestigious job. For others it means spending less time at work and more time with their family. For other people it could be stepping down from positions that made them feel good about themselves and taking on roles that are less popular, more difficult, or "less important."

You simply cannot do everything, and as you start to identify your primary areas of influence, you will have to make some difficult decisions about how to make room for them. But this is one of those paradoxes of life: As you relinquish control of particular areas, your influence will actually expand. Consider how you can influence your environment from your given position? And, what are the opportunities in front of you that seem to be uniquely *your* opportunities?

One of my favorite authors encourages his readers, when facing scary, risky, difficult choices that are full of great possibilities, to imagine themselves going for it and then asking themselves:

What if you hadn't?

Think back on some of the greatest successes our society has experienced. They came about because of courageous choices. Think of political leaders, business leaders, community leaders, normal everyday people who impacted change that has shaped our lives for the better because they had the courage to choose to move forward with their ideas.

The difference between influencers and non-influencers is that people who don't influence run away from risk because they fear failing. Influencers run toward risk because they fear missing the opportunity.

What are the opportunities in front of you? What change can you make in your family, in your community, in your organization? Fast forward to the day when that becomes a reality and ask yourself:

What if you hadn't?

Now, what do you need to do?

I began this book with a story about me traveling to Kurdistan and then Afghanistan because opportunity presented itself and I had a background and a skill set that might matter to people in the area. There was a plan in place when I left. Some of that plan was implemented, but much of what happened was a result of dealing with the emergent work I was presented with in both countries. When I left, I had only a loose idea of what success might look like. I came home with stories I never expected to be part of.

"The difference between influencers and non-influencers is that people who don't influence run away from risk because they fear failing. Influencers run toward risk because they fear missing the opportunity."

My favorite involves a young man named Javid, who is now a friend of my family:

When in Herat teaching, I met Javid. Javid was a student in one of the classes I taught and he stood out to me because during one exercise he was willing to join a group of young women in order to balance the number of people in various groups. A small thing, but it caused me to catch up with him after class and ask him why he did that. It turns out he has a sister and he's just not that tied to some of the cultural norms that might have caused others to be nervous about sitting with a group of young women. We chatted a bit and spoke again the next day but then the bomb hit and I wasn't able to get back to morning classes at the university. I didn't think much more about Javid until I returned to the U.S. and received a Facebook invite from him (along with a few other classmates of his). Javid also "friended" my son and daughter who are close to his age. True to my generation, I was reluctant to join the Facebook masses, but now am a happy user. Technology has enabled me to expand community in beautiful ways.

Javid is an ambitious and high-potential young man. He wants his home country to be strong and he believes his generation can lead and make changes. He had a vision to come to the US for school and then return to Afghanistan to teach. My daughter, Elizabeth, helped Javid edit some of the work he did to apply for scholarships to come to school in the U.S. His hard work and bright mind caught the attention of several organizations and Javid is now a student at a university in Oregon.

With no family nearby and no resources to travel to his home in Herat, I invited Javid to spend his first Christmas break in Colorado with my family. He accepted and we enjoyed a week of special time sharing traditions, playing in the snow and discussing how small the world has become.

My family saw Javid spread his prayer rug and kneel to the east. Javid joined my family at a candle light Christmas Eve service were we sang *Silent Night*. It struck me that the silent night we sang about in church occurred a couple thousand years ago not far from Javid's home.

Javid and my family will remain in touch and will be in relationship. What will happen beyond that? I have no clue. I'm hopeful Javid will remain true to his vision and be a leader in a part of the world that desperately needs people with his vision, compassion and intelligence. But there's really no way to know if that will happen or not. What I do know is that people who press in to life and examine themselves – who determine their Character, their Community and then make the Choice to act will live big lives.

Part of the human condition is to talk about great ideas but then rarely do anything about them.

You're probably already doing a lot of the foundational elements we've talked about in this book. You could tell us all about your week, what your life looks like, and how you approach a Monday morning. You could talk to us about various interactions you've had recently that have peaked your curiosity, meetings you've had with new people that seem to be tugging you in a new direction. But are you going after the change you know is needed in your company, your community?

You could walk us through what your funeral will look like, who will talk, what they'll say, and who will carry your coffin. We could dream together about what people will be saying about you 30 years down the road. But are you intentionally going after the vision of your life?

This book isn't a call to conquer a nation as much as it is a call to engage your community, find out what you have to do, and then go do it. Small steps. Little daily choices spread out over decades. Choices that start out as small ripples and eventually turn into large waves. And in time...

- Your influence will increase.

- Your impact will deepen.

- Those in your community will be impacted and inspired.

Now, go do.

***

Andy Stanley, author of *Visioneering*, writes, "Vision is a clear mental picture of what could be, fueled by the conviction that it should be." Hopefully you've begun creating a vision not only of how to make your organization or community better, but also how you want you and your future to be better.

I wrote earlier about Lincoln, Gandhi, and Mandela. They didn't have an easy path to walk, and you won't either, but we all have to take our journeys one step at a time. Step by step. Moment by moment.

Don't get discouraged.

Stay the course.

Do the next thing in front of you.

Then the next thing. Then the next.

Now it's time.

Go do.

LIFT

Acknowledgments

Lift is the first book I've written and going through the process, particularly at the end when it's time to press "Enter" for the final time, feels like standing naked in the town square and asking people to make comments. There is no opportunity to shade meaning, pretend to have said something else or be shy about making a statement – it's all out there for the world to see. Writing the book took longer than I expected in part because it's easier to think thoughts than it is to write words and in part because "life" had a way of raising its hand and demanding attention. Looking back on the process, there's no way the book would have happened without the efforts of many people.

Betsy Nichols is one of those people you might encounter first while sitting in an audience when she's speaking. You'd think, "what an interesting, cool young woman!" You would be precisely correct. Betsy is a joy to know, a bright business associate and life-giving as a community member. Much of the book is owed to Betsy's insight and her willingness to challenge me and others to find the best and not settle for good.

Shawn Smucker got me started by laying a solid foundation for the structure of Lift.

Walter McFarland easily played the role of "smartest guy in the room" and willingly offered me comments, thoughts and time.

Ross Paterson walked (and rode) with me through the book and served as "Cycling Editor."

My friends and associates from Coaching and Consulting for Change – especially Denis Bourgeois. You opened my eyes to new ways to view human behavior and, in the process, made me more human.

My friends and co-workers at Symbolist. Thanks for being excellent.

Author Bio

Tom Miller is founder and President of Symbolist, a management consulting firm specializing in employee engagement and cultural communication. As a consultant and advisor, he has worked with major corporations to build systems that strengthen culture and engagement. He is a regular speaker and writer. To learn more about Tom and Symbolist, please visit www.symbolist.com.

A strategic publisher empowering authors to strengthen their brand.

Visit Elevate Publishing for our latest offerings.
www.elevatepub.com

NO TREES WERE HARMED
IN THE MAKING OF THIS BOOK

OK, so a few
did need to make the ultimate sacrifice.

In order to steward our environment,
we are partnering with *Plant With Purpose*, to plant
a tree for every tree that paid the price for the printing of
this book.

$\Longrightarrow$ PLANT W TH PURPOSE

www.plantwithpurpose.org

go to www.elevatepub.com/about to learn more

CPSIA information can be obtained at www.ICGtesting.com
Printed in the USA
BVOW06*2343240116

434065BV00016B/152/P